D1433927

THE STRIKE

THE STRIKE

An Insider's Story

Roy Ottey

SIDGWICK & JACKSON

LONDON

I wish to express gratitude to Peter Davis, a North Staffordshire journalist, for his help, guidance, research and particularly his motivation, without which this book would probably never have been completed.

First published in Great Britain in 1985
by Sidgwick & Jackson Limited

ISBN: 0-283-99228-X

Typeset by Tellgate Ltd, London WC1
Printed in Great Britain by
The Garden City Press, Letchworth, Hertfordshire
for Sidgwick & Jackson Limited
1 Tavistock Chambers, Bloomsbury Way
London, WC1A 2SG

For Doris,
and for miners everywhere

List of Plates

Contents

The Principal Characters

Trevor Bell Right-wing General Secretary of the Colliery Officials and Staffs' Association area. Was a leading contender for the national presidency against Arthur Scargill. A close colleague of mine, he has given great service to the union and is a very good administrator.

Owen Briscoe Left-wing Yorkshire General Secretary. Very provocative, and enjoys the cut and thrust of debate in Executive meetings.

Gilbert Butler Left-wing General Secretary of North Derbyshire where he succeeded Peter Heathfield. Direct in his observations, he always has something to say. Very smart, he is one of the best-dressed men on the NUM Executive.

Ray Chadburn Nottinghamshire area President. Right-wing, he stood against Arthur Scargill in the presidential election. I thought at one time he would go to the top in the union but perhaps his ambition does not match his obvious ability. I have always got on well with Ray. Outside the union he is, like me, a keen gardener.

Wesley Chambers A left-wing member of the Executive for Kent, but not a fulltime official. Round-faced and fresh-looking, he is a friendly man and one of his main interests outside the union is photography, which is something I am also interested in. However, we don't see eye to eye politically.

Eric Clarke Left-wing General Secretary, Scotland. Totally committed to the left. Never appears to be worried, is a very jovial man, but can be very cutting with some of his remarks.

Jim Colgan Left-wing General Secretary of the right-wing Midlands area. A comparative newcomer to the Executive, he is a strong Scargill supporter. Always seems to have the welfare of his men at heart but appears to be torn between support for the left wing and support for his own area.

Ron Dunn A right-winger, who represents Durham and Northumberland craftsmen on the Executive. A man of few words but able to put over his point of view.

Joe Gormley An able negotiator, who boosted the miners' earnings to the top of the industrial wages league, he was President of the NUM from 1971 to 1982. He led the miners' strikes of 1972 and 1974, the latter resulting in the downfall of the Heath Government. An excellent speaker and a good friend, he is a jovial character with whom I have spent many happy hours.

Harry Hanlon Right-wing General Secretary of the Cumberland area. A lively personality who always has a dry comment on the tip of his tongue. Easy-going and always pleasant towards me.

Peter Heathfield Elected General Secretary of the NUM in 1984. Formerly General Secretary of the North Derbyshire area. Deeply committed to the left wing, he likes to analyse situations. He will go to the rostrum, take apart all the implications of a resolution and examine each point. He always seems contented and has been consistently friendly towards me.

Jack Jones Right-wing General Secretary of the Leicestershire area, not to be confused with Jack Jones, former General Secretary of the TGWU. A dedicated union man, he is always ready to press home his point of view, and that of his members.

An ex-Navy man, whenever he sends a Christmas or birthday card to my home, he always signs it 'sailor'.

Ian MacGregor A naturalized American who became Chairman of the National Coal Board in 1983, having previously been Chairman of the British Steel Corporation. He was not my choice for Chairman, and it was obvious from day one that his appointment would create friction. I always found him to be an approachable man, who was determined to make the industry profitable.

Mick McGahey Vice-President of the NUM and Communist President of his own Scottish area. He is the man I always regarded as the driving force behind Arthur Scargill. I admire his ability to play on the emotions of the crowd when addressing rallies. An outgoing person who enjoys a drink and a laugh, he is someone I would like to have had on our side, and I often asked him: 'Why are you a Communist, Mick?' But I never seemed to get a satisfactory answer. Before I resigned I gave him a Doulton wall plaque of the Houses of Parliament. I was pleased to be able to say it had belonged to my father, who had at one time been known as 'Bolshevik Joe'.

Ted McKay Right-wing General Secretary of the North Wales area. His area was split during the strike and he had a particularly difficult time and was forced to move out of his home because of threats. A genuine person who will always be my friend.

Abe Moffat Left-wing Scottish craftsmen's leader, and son of illustrious Scottish miners' leader. Very friendly with Mick McGahey and a strong supporter of the militants.

Idwal Morgan Left-wing General Secretary of the Cokemen's area. A Welshman, he is a firm Scargill supporter. His predecessor was right-wing and Idwal seemed to change the area's policy attitude overnight when he was elected to the Executive in 1984. A forceful speaker, but not a very tolerant man; he doesn't seem to like people who disagree with him.

Denis Murphy   Right-wing President of the Northumberland area. Very popular, happy-go-lucky man who can be blunt and outspoken. We have had lots of laughs together and I can still picture him outside a Peking hotel marching up and down as though he was on guard duty, with a broom over his shoulder. Has the gift of cheering everybody up.

George Rees   Left-wing General Secretary of South Wales. A tough man but outgoing and friendly. Not afraid to speak his mind and is quick to argue with Arthur Scargill when he doesn't agree with him.

Henry Richardson   Left-wing General Secretary in right-wing Nottinghamshire area. Was suspended from office by his own area during the strike for opposing the area's breakaway move from the NUM. Serious-minded, he called for a ballot in the early days of the strike. Despite his left-wing tendencies, he always hammered home his members' point of view, and I respect him for that.

Arthur Scargill   President of the National Union of Mineworkers. Started on his road to 'stardom' back in 1969 during an unofficial strike in Yorkshire. Later became President of the Yorkshire area and was elected leader of the NUM in 1981 with a massive 70.3 per cent vote. He never compromises, even when I think he should do in the best interests of his members. Always believes he is right. He is a brilliant speaker, but I regard his political views as a danger to democracy within the union. A hard-working individual and virtually a teetotaller, he can also be a very caring person. He seemed genuinely concerned when my wife Doris was seriously ill, and often enquired about her health. Sometimes, though, he seems to be in a world of his own. Delegates assembling for meetings have been heard to say, rather snidely: 'I wonder if anyone's given the key in his back a turn?'

Bill Stobbs   Left-winger, branch lodge chairman at Easington Colliery, Durham. Not a fulltime official, he doesn't have a lot to say for himself. Simply makes his point and leaves it at that.

Jack Taylor   Left-wing Yorkshire President who succeeded Arthur Scargill, leader of the union's largest area. Typical blunt Yorkshireman, he is a pleasant man socially and has a good sense of humour. Not as left-wing as some of his colleagues, he is an able organizer.

Ken Toon   Right-wing South Derbyshire General Secretary. Elder statesman of the Executive and a very good friend of mine. Has weathered some difficult situations in his time and was the first to back the introduction of the incentive scheme in the industry.

Sid Vincent   Right-wing General Secretary of the North Western (Lancashire) area. A down-to-earth union man who argued strongly for a ballot early in the strike, and a great character; I have always got on well with him. I will always remember how during a miners' delegation visit to China he had everyone rolling about with laughter as he sang his own version of a George Formby song to a Chinese interpreter named Mrs Wu. He has a marvellous singing voice and was always the star turn at union social events.

Johnny Weaver   A left-winger from Yorkshire. Not a full-time official but is a strong supporter of Yorkshire policy. One of the most popular members of the Executive, he has the sort of face that seems to smile at you all the time.

Emlyn Williams   Left-wing President of South Wales. A powerful, marvellous speaker at the rostrum. We were friendly to each other but invariably held opposing points of view.

Fanning the Flames

I could almost smell the hate as I gazed upon the angry crowd of strikers waiting for me outside Silverdale Colliery social club in North Staffordshire. It was 29 March 1984 and the miners' strike was entering its fourth week. Shouts of 'traitor' and 'scab' filled the air as I emerged from the club and started to manoeuvre apprehensively past the jostling bodies, expecting at any moment to feel someone's fist crashing against my face.

It was a terrifying experience – degrading too. One miner started to spit and others joined in. Another called me a bastard and pushed his face within a few inches of mine. I shall never forget his face: it was distorted with rage.

'Keep going . . . if they kill me, they kill me,' I quietly repeated to myself. I refused to show fear and I knew I must not hesitate. It was just a short walk to the car, but it seemed endless.

That day still haunts me: it all seemed so unreal. I was a National Union of Mineworkers' official campaigning for democracy within the union, but some of the men I was trying to help had turned against me and called me traitor.

My crime was that two days earlier I had organized a meeting of the right wing of the NUM Executive in an attempt to force a ballot over the strike. It was my misfortune that my Press statement was cut short on television. Everyone thought I was advising men to cross picket lines when, in fact, the opposite was the case.

What later became known as the 'secret public meeting' involved seven other NUM moderate leaders and was held at a hotel near Leicester on 27 March. It sparked off a series of frightening events which I will probably recall every day of the rest of my life.

Angry strikers lobbied my office and screamed abuse at me; there were threats on my life and the CID offered me police protection; protesting miners, the worse for drink, cornered me after a meeting, prodding me with their beer glasses and murmuring obscenities while others deflated the tyres of my car in a bid to prevent me getting away.

The strike had just begun and many of us still clung to the hope that the mineworkers would be given their national ballot as was their right within the union rule book. I was determined to do my best to get them a ballot, and to do what I could to wrestle the power away from the few militants who were leading our great union into civil war.

I was shunned by men I once regarded as my friends. I was labelled a 'scab' and there were calls for my resignation. But I knew that the strike was wrong. It was undemocratic.

One miner was reported in the Press as saying: 'He should support the NUM or resign. All he can do is hold clandestine meetings.'

And there was another who said: 'A majority of men across the country now support the strike – but Roy Ottey will not accept this.'

That was true. I would not accept it was a national strike when, in fact, it was not.

But it was not true that the majority of men supported it. I believe that only a minority backed the strike. Thousands stayed at home because they were afraid to go to work. Those who did brave the picket lines, particularly in the early days of the dispute, faced threats and abuse, and many were assaulted.

I was encouraged by statements made by some of my colleagues in the craftsmen's Power Group. Our Vice-President, Jim Dowling, stated in the local evening paper that he had been contacted by pitmen who wanted to organize a counter-demonstration in support of me.

'I have had many calls both from our craftsmen and also miners saying that they are in favour of his action,' he said.

And another leading Power Group figure, the winding engineers' secretary, Steve Higginson, said: 'We fully endorse the action that Roy Ottey took in trying to get a ballot vote. This is the only democratic way to resolve this issue.'

I thanked them but had to admit to a feeling of inadequacy. I felt that no matter what I did, the strike would run its course and the union would be split wide open.

As I listened to the chanting, protesting crowd, I wondered if all the insults and threats were worth suffering. I could easily have kept my mouth shut and let events take their course without bothering to represent the craftsmen fully.

But I knew I would never have forgiven myself if I had taken the easy way out. I walked on, praying nothing would happen before I reached the car . . . .

– 1 –
Early Life

I was born in the small mining village of Battram, Leicester-shire, on 8 November 1924. My earliest recollection, though it may seem hard to believe, is of being pushed in the pram to a shop to buy fireworks.

Next, I can remember my father, who was a miner, sitting in the blazing sunshine playing cards at an upturned beer barrel which was used to catch rainwater for us to wash in. It was 1926: the year of the General Strike. Father had been on strike since it began in early May that year. Although the various trade unionists who had come out in sympathy had gone back to work by mid-May, the miners stayed out until November of that year.

Father seemed to spend his whole time sitting at the beer barrel playing cards, staking bets with matches. To this day matches seem important – more important even than money. We certainly didn't have any of that in those days: that was why my father used to walk all the way to Coalville, four and a half miles away, in the hope of collecting something from the various gifts of clothing, shoes and other provisions sent to the Strike Centre to relieve the hardship of the striking miners. Often, though, he came home empty-handed, saying to my mother who was distraught with worry about how we would survive the strike: 'It was all rubbish. There were holes in the shoes!'

We lived in a tiny terraced house, two up, two down. The rooms were only eight feet square. I used to share a bedroom with my sister, Joyce. When my brother John was born, he had to sleep in my mother's room.

Onto the scene comes Grandad Ottey. He didn't work any longer, and years of working down the mines in water meant that his legs only moved from the knees down: the upper half was frozen stiff. He always walked with a stick with a hook on the end, and had an infuriating habit of poking me with it, saying: 'Are you all right, teapot? [That was his nickname for me which I hated.] What you been crying for?' The thought of where that stick had been – he used to claim that he picked slugs and snails out of the grass on the roadside and popped them into his mouth – filled me with horror.

I could never understand why, when we were so hard-up, some of our neighbours were comparatively rich. Then one day I discovered that our neighbour, Mr Preston, was 'scabbing' and going to work every day as a winding engineman – the person who operated the big engine that sent the cages up and down the shaft at the pit.

Sometimes, though, I personally would contribute to the household budget, for the directors of the local colliery used to come now and again for a day's shooting in the woods, and the gamekeepers would ask the lads in the village to act as beaters.

Mam would be up early in order to get me ready. She used to cut strips of brown paper, wrap them round and round my legs and then tie them with string. In theory, this was to keep my legs dry; but by the end of the day, it was a soggy mess. Still, there was no money for Wellingtons: only rich people had them.

Mam was always pleased when I handed over the shilling for the day's work. I used to hope that this would perhaps stop her going every morning to clean at the pub. I hated her doing that. I shall never forget her knees which were black and crinkled and hard, like corns, from kneeling to scrub the floor.

Then after the strike ended and we had a little more money, an unforgettable event occurred: an electrician came and put wires in the little living-room and in Mam and Dad's bedroom. No more walking to the neighbouring village to fetch paraffin for the brass lamp in the middle of the ceiling! No more having to put up with the terrible smell the wick gave off as it blackened the ceiling with smoke!

Schooldays started. Though we only had one new set of

clothes each year, Mam was a stickler for cleanliness and looking smart. Every day before setting out for school we had to
have a bath. Father filled the boiler at the side of the black-
leaded grate with rainwater from the beer barrel, and the zinc
bath in front of the fire filled up with hot and cold water, complete with little red and black tadpoles. Sometimes too there
was soot floating on the top which had come down the chimney
into the boiler.

I enjoyed school. My father had always loved studying: he
still went to night school and he positively encouraged learning. But, of course, there was no money for books: *Sinbad the
Sailor* and *A Tale of Two Cities* are the only two books I
remember reading. Father had always been active in the Wes-
leyan Reform Chapel, and Sundays were spent listening to
stories which filled me with wonder, and learning to read from
the Bible.

Though life was still coloured by what I felt was great deprivation, things were getting slightly better. The landlord of the
pub, who also owned the house we lived in, had coal-houses and
proper lavatories built. This meant that the house was clear of
coal and we didn't any longer have to share the lavatory fifty
yards down the yard. It was heaven. The lavatory man used to
come in the middle of night with his horsedrawn tub on wheels
and empty the pans, his way lit by carbide lamps with bullseye
glasses, fitted either side of the shafts.

Then one day a great calamity befell us: Dad lost his job. He
had been sacked – for 'filling with the shovel'.

In those days, the coal was won from the face by the men
hacking away at the base of the coal and creating a gap at the
bottom. This technique was called 'hand-holing'. Then they
would hand-grind a hole in the top of the coal and fill it with
powder before a fireman blasted it down. They would then fill
the coal into tubs on wheels, which were brought to the face by
pony-drivers. The mine owners, however, only wanted coal of a
certain size, and so the men had to fill the tubs first, using a
fork with large-spaced tines.

Because they were paid on tonnage, they took chances on
occasions by filling with a shovel instead of the fork. Of course,

this meant that coal in various sizes ended up in the tub. If the deputy (the man in charge of the coalface) or pit manager suspected, they would have the tub turned over to inspect the contents and, even if they were wrong, the men had to fill it again for no extra money. In my father's case, the manager had suspected correctly.

Luck, however, eventually smiled on us: father apologized to the manager and was given his job back.

At the age of fourteen, I left school and found a job in a shoe factory, putting milky-white glue on the leather soles of shoes. It wasn't very interesting, and it was a long day having to travel twelve miles by bus, starting at 8am and leaving at 6pm. All for ten shillings and sixpence a week. Just four days later I was offered a job making up orders in a yarn store at Wolsey. That lasted about six months. I thought I had done rather well, but the manager thought another job, other than making up orders of yarn, might suit me better. So it was back to another shoe factory, at Earl Shilton this time, a bit nearer home. To liven up the job of sticking soles on shoes, we used to discuss matters of the day across the table. Sometimes, though, this led to arguments, and I clearly remember one of my mates, head and shoulders taller than me, throwing down his brushes and lifting his fists to strike me. I couldn't resist the challenge. There were, I think, only two blows which landed actually on me. Mother noticed the swelling and the black eye when I got home. Father just laughed. I determined that, henceforth, discretion would be the better part of valour.

The next date I remember clearly is 3 September 1939. It was a Sunday, and I was now fifteen years old. I had been out pedalling around the countryside with a mate on my newly-acquired bike. We stopped to speak to some friends who were sitting on the pavement outside their houses, and suddenly there was an announcement on the radio. We listened with bated breath as the Prime Minister, Neville Chamberlain, announced: 'As from 11 o'clock this morning we are at war with Germany.'

I was astride the bike almost before he finished, pedalling faster than ever before, fully expecting that at any minute Germans would appear.

I remember my father saying one day: 'I'll tell you what —
Hitler's done something good for us; we're working regular
now, and they want the coal so much, they're talking about us
working on Saturdays.'

A chord struck in my head: if they want more coal, they will
want more men, I reasoned silently. I was spurred on by the
knowledge that pit lads earned seventeen shillings a week. On
the other hand I knew what my father's attitude would be: no
way was he going to see his son be a pit man! There had to be a
better job for him than that!

Next morning, however, I feigned sickness so as not to go to
work. Then, when mother had gone out to clean, I got up, put on
my best suit and walked up to the pit, past the row of tiny little
houses sitting virtually in the pit-yard, behind which coal
wagons were loaded. I went through the yard, all coal-dust and
sludge.

My heart in my mouth, I knocked at the door of the manager's office.

'Come in,' said a quiet voice.

'I'm Roy Ottey,' I explained. 'I'd like a job. I'm working in a
shoe factory at Earl Shilton and it's a long way to travel. I'd like
to be on the surface, please.'

'There's no such thing as a surface job,' he grunted. 'If you
want a job, you go down pit.'

Plaintively I said, 'Yes sir, thank you, sir.'

The interview had ended, and he hadn't even looked at me.

'I don't know what your father will say, our Roy,' said mother
when I told her. 'You know he didn't want you to go to pit; you
should have a better job than that.'

Eventually I plucked up the courage to tell him. Just as I
thought, he flew into a rage; I thought he was going to kill me!
He started flailing his arms about and the words flowed so
thick and fast I don't remember what he said. But by later that
night he had, apparently, accepted my decision as irreversible,
for he said: 'Billy [a neighbour who worked as a fitter in the pit]
is going to ask in the morning if they want any lads in the
shops. It'll be better than going down pit.'

So the next evening I went straight past the pit and the manager's office and went up to a large semi-detached house. I was met by Mr Bailey, the man responsible for employing electricians. He looked at me quizzically and then, bending down to pick up a stick, handed it to me with the words: 'Draw me a bell circuit on the ground.'

I couldn't have been luckier; it was one of the things we had learned in the last weeks of school. Standing in the evening sunshine I drew the circuit in the dusty garden soil.

'Tell me how it works,' he said.

I explained. I must have been right, for he asked me to report to the electricians' shop at half-past six the following Monday.

That morning I was up earlier than ever. For the first time I put on pit-boots, which with their heavy soles felt like lead weights on the ends of my legs. Father started to give his last-minute instructions: 'What you do at the pit reflects on me and your Mam. Do as you're told and work hard. And another thing, go and see George Harry Brearley in the carpenters' shop. He's the union man for the shopmen. Don't come home tonight if you haven't joined.'

I walked into the electricians' shop, feeling strange and out of place. But I was determined to heed Father's words, and so carried out my supervisor's instructions, running hither and thither to fetch and carry, handing him the right tools from the heavy tool bag I carried for him. At breakfast-time I announced that I wanted to join the union. One of the men grinned and said: 'Oh, ah! Bolshevik Joe, eh?' I didn't really know what he meant, but I understood that this was an allusion to my father and had something to do with the 1926 strike.

I went to see George at midday when we stopped for sandwiches.

'So you want to join the union?' he said, scrabbling about beneath his bench in a cupboard.

'Yes please,' said I.

He came out from beneath the bench with a yellow card and, with his big oily hands, scribbled 'Roy Ottey' at the top and ticked a space.

'That'll be threepence ha'penny a week,' he said. 'You're only a juvenile. It'll be sevenpence when you're eighteen.'

That was it. Later that day I explained the happenings of the day to Father. The next night he announced that a Workers' Educational Association meeting was held on Tuesday nights, and that he and I would be going.

Something clicked. Looking back I suppose I thought that if I was going to pay threepence ha'penny out of my wages every week, then I ought to know where it went. So, week after week, Father and I would walk the mile to the meeting. On the way, he would air his views on capitalism, socialism and the economy.

Meanwhile, my three workmates, who were all older than me, had taken me under their wing, insisted that I join the Association of Mining, Mechanical and Electrical Engineers, and kept sweeping me off to union meetings with them.

Days in the pit were long and exhausting. I would walk home coated with coal-dust, looking like a black African, and it was a terrible job trying to get clean in the zinc bath. My eyes would have black rings round them, where the coal-dust was stuck in the lashes, for days at a time. Later we discovered that rubbing olive oil into the eyelids before washing cleanly removed the dust.

But life didn't only revolve around work. I also had my eye on a lovely girl called Doris – later to become my wife. With her peaches and cream complexion and long brown hair, it was love at first sight. I took her to the Regal cinema to see films like *Love on the Dole* and finally she invited me home for supper. I remember we ate bread and butter, cheese and cake and piccalilli. The last was so hot it brought tears to my eyes. My meeting Doris was the beginning of a rewarding and constantly loving companionship that continues today.

The war had now impinged on everyone's life in one way or another. Rationing was in full swing and food was short. As an economy measure, my family had decided to keep a pig in the back garden. When it was fat enough, the pig-killer, Dinkler Farmer, would be commissioned to come and kill it. He would arrive early in the morning, leather apron tied around his waist, sharpening his many knives with deft movements on a block of steel.

I never liked the squeals of the pig, which seemed to go on and on until the last drop of blood had oozed from its neck. I would catch this in a large basin, called a panchin, and stir it continuously to stop it congealing. This was used for making black pudding. Then there were the intestines which, once stuffed with belly meat, made delicious sausages. Finally the carcass was hung by the back legs and cut up into shoulders, hams and sides which were taken into the pantry, laid on the thrall – a concrete slab – rubbed with salt, and left to cure.

Meantime I was getting more and more involved in union matters. I was now a member of the National Union of Enginemen, Firemen, Mechanics and Electrical Workers: its members were drawn from any industry where machinery was operated or maintained. This union was originally founded in 1892 but in 1923 it amalgamated with the Transport and General Workers' Union. This became known as the 1923 Agreement. At the time, however, it was decided that, unlike other small unions which amalgamated with the TGWU, the NUEFMEW would be separately registered and known as the Power Group. Many of our members were, of course, miners and this meant that the same union also became the Power Group section of the Miners' Federation of Great Britain.

My regular attendance at branch meetings of the union had, apparently, been observed, as had my ability to remember, virtually word for word, the precise details of agreement reached with the coal-owners. It was certainly a proud moment for me when I learnt that I had been nominated, seconded and elected President of the branch – a position which I held for the next two years.

It was not until 1944 that the National Union of Mineworkers came into being. It was founded in Nottingham during a conference of the Miners' Federation of Great Britain. Many of the delegates could, of course, remember the General Strike of 1926 and the traumas and deprivations which accompanied it. They wanted to ensure that, by becoming part of the NUM, they would not be sacrificing the individual members' democratic rights: never again did they want to let miners and their families suffer deprivation as they had in 1926, unless they opted to do so in a ballot vote. I felt proud to be part of the NUM, with its carefully thought-out constitution and rules.

Father and I were still attending Workers' Educational Association meetings once a week. There we discussed everything on the political scene, including the Labour Government and nationalization, in particular the nationalization of the mines. Father had already presented me with a Labour Party membership card; his fervency for social change had now become a fervent belief in democratic socialism: not for him any ideology which might thwart freedom of expression, whether it be personal or political. I latched on to his every word – I think at the time I really did believe he was infallible.

On 18 May 1946 Doris and I were married. A six-roomed house suddenly became vacant in Co-op Row, so named because it faced the Co-op shop in Bagworth, and it was offered to me. Though management were prepared to make an exception in my case, it was considered unfair for the house to be offered to a single man. Quick as a flash, I rectified that by asking Doris, 'the beautiful one' as I called her, to marry me. Friends and relations helped supply furniture for the house, and Father and a friend donated a ham and a barrel of beer for the reception in Co-op Hall after the ceremony. With our house in Co-op Row and a few pounds in the bank, Doris and I wanted little else: we had each other.

On 1 January 1947 came the eagerly awaited nationalization of the mining industry. We had long considered this an absolute must for miners and on the inaugural day – 'vesting day' as it was known – we anticipated all sorts of wonderful things. The pits were to become ours at last!

A flagpole, glistening white, had been erected just inside the pit gates at Bagworth. We had decided that Bill Hooton, who was over seventy and the oldest working man, would have the honour of raising the flag on this historic day.

The morning came and we collected around the pole. We waited and waited. Nothing could happen until Mr Neath, the manager, gave the signal. Suddenly, he strode from his little office and, without a glimmer of a smile, said: 'Pull the flag, Bill.' I sensed Mr Neath was not too happy about the event.

The flag started up the pole, thereby exposing a blue-painted board, fixed to the wall, with white-painted letters proclaiming 'This Colliery is now managed by the National Coal Board on behalf of the people'. At the top the flag unfurled to reveal the letters 'NCB'. We all clapped.

Shortly after, I was told that there was to be considerable mechanization of the pits, and I was sent to Sheffield to learn about the new machinery. What I learnt there stood me in good stead for future developments in the industry. At about the same time, Pit Production Committees came into being to help determine production targets and act as a forum for discussions about general welfare. Having now relinquished my position as President of the union branch, I was free to enter my first election at the pit for the position of representative of the tradesmen on this new committee. Subsequently the only other candidate thinking of running withdrew in my favour, leaving me to walk into the job. It led to my belonging to many other committees, and at last we saw conditions at the pit really improve: we had canteens and pithead baths; gone were the days of having to go home to get clean in the zinc bath with tadpoles.

Mechanization of the pits came slowly, but the sense of achievement was tremendous when, with a coal-face nearly exhausted, fitters and electricians would organize the transfer of all the machinery, with cables, transformers and switches, to the new face which might be a mile or so away. Spanners flying, screwdrivers whirling, the machines would be dismantled into transportable sections, loaded onto flat trolleys and drawn to the new district by rope haulage. Cables, in hundred-yard lengths, were split at the joints and dragged by chain on the same rope haulage into the new position.

At the start of production on Monday morning we were there to watch the men crawl onto the face. Everything then sprang into electrical and mechanical life, as the coal spewed off the loader and filled the tubs. We had done our job well. The miners could now do likewise.

In 1956 I was selected, I know not how or by whom, to represent the Leicestershire area at the National Coal Board summer school, held in Oxford. Various high-ranking members of the NCB came to speak, providing us with an opportunity to discuss and air our opinions on any aspect at all of the industry's activity. By this time I was representing the tradesmen at the pit on the Consultative Committee, which had replaced the Production Committee and allowed us even greater participation in all affairs of the pit.

Then, three years later, I learnt that our District Secretary, Bill Edge, had died suddenly. One of two assistants was bound to be promoted to fill his job, leaving a vacancy for an assistant based in the district office in Stoke-on-Trent. I remember one of the lads coming up to me and saying, 'We want you for that job, Roy. How about it?'

'How would you like to live in Stoke-on-Trent?' I asked my wife later that day.

'What, that dirty hole!' was her initial reaction. But then, when I related the details of the job, she said: 'Well,' with typical female logic, 'if you don't apply for the job, you won't get it.'

We said no more; I simply reported the conversation to the lads next morning when they arrived for the day shift, and at the next branch meeting my nomination was accepted.

All nominated candidates had to be interviewed by the Executive Council, which was composed of members from the various districts of the union. Questions would be wide-ranging, spanning the industries – mining, electricity supply, steel, gas, water, sugar, cement, as well as the Mersey Docks and Harbour Board, Ford Motor Company, and Royal Ordnance factories – and moving on to social security benefits and regulations, the union rule book, conciliation procedures and the Trade Union Congress, the Labour Party and international trade union organizations.

The following weeks were hectic; Doris sat with various pamphlets, books and documents before her, testing me on them, while at work I stuffed books down the front of my overalls so that I could read as I walked down the pit or during mealtimes – 'snapping time' we called it.

When the interview day came, I knew not how I had fared, but I had at least given an answer to all the questions, right or wrong. However, I soon learnt that I was one of two shortlisted.

The other selected candidate and I now had to appear before representatives of all the branches in the district. We would each speak for a given period and then answer questions from the floor. The representatives from all the industries would subsequently go back and advise their members how they should vote.

I drove to the conference at the Borough Hall, Stafford on a foggy, murky and rainy Saturday night. On the way I took a wrong turning, reversed into a pub entrance, struck a concrete post holding a chain link fence and ended up crunching the back bumper and bootlid of the car. Not easily deterred, I drove on to the conference. I was, it seems, much more adept at answering questions that night than driving, for on 20 February 1959 I received an official letter, offering me the job. I was thirty-four, the youngest officer the union had ever had.

Shortly after I was asked to travel to London to meet the General Secretary, Bill Tudor, at his office in Transport House, the headquarters of the Transport and General Workers' Union. Only having been to London twice before – once to savour celebrations for the Festival of Britain in 1951 and once to visit Earls Court to see an exhibition of mining machinery – I was somewhat apprehensive about the meeting.

However, my apprehension disappeared when, arriving at Transport House, an imposing red-brick building in Smith Square, Westminster, I met Bill Tudor. He was sitting in an office he shared with a bronze bust of the man who founded the TGWU, Ernest Bevin, and greeted me in a warm, friendly way. Bill was a large, most affable man, an ex-docker and sometime wrestler and, as General Secretary, was our union representative on the NUM Executive. In the past I had crossed swords with him, especially on the matter of whether craftsmen got the recognition and remuneration they deserved. But all that was now forgotten as we discussed how and where I should fit into the organization. He told me that I could stay in my home at Bagworth, operating for the membership in that half of the district but still under the jurisdiction of the district secretary. I would not actually have any office facilities: obviously, I would need a telephone, but it would have to be installed at my own expense, although I could register my calls on behalf of the union, and claim at the month's end. The situation was hardly ideal, but I was relieved that I would not have to move from Stoke-on-Trent, and I recognized that the union I had now become a more influential part of was far from rich.

On the other hand, there were some compensations. For example, I now found myself meeting people I had previously only known by reputation, like the 'big boss', Bill Unsworth, who was the South Midlands area general manager of the NCB and lived in a bungalow in the grounds of a massive hall with enormous gardens, bought by the NCB as the area headquarters in the early days of nationalization, much to the disgust of local miners. I also met the Secretary of the Leicestershire miners and a member of the NUM Executive, Frank Smith. In the streets of Coalville he was instantly recognizable for he had an Errol Flynn moustache, wore spats and carried a rolled umbrella. I admired him very much and he reinforced me in my conviction that the members were the union, not us, and that democracy and democratic rights were of paramount importance in our society.

The next few years saw many changes. To begin with, I had to go to the office in Hanley, Staffordshire, at least once a week. How I wished when I got there that I knew something about office work! The office secretary, a young dumpy girl with a moon-shaped face and eyes so big they seemed to encompass you completely, would come to take dictation, sitting down opposite me and looking at me expectantly, book and pencil at the ready. It was months before I could dictate spontaneously, and at the start I suffered a great deal of embarrassment, watching her eyes widen in anticipation as I dictated, for example, the gory details of accidents which had left men impotent.

In 1959 I attended my first union conference. It was the TGWU Biennial Delegate Conference on the Isle of Man and, though I was allowed time off work, I had to pay my own way there. It was worth it though, for I found it an exhilarating experience and educational into the bargain. The great debate of the week was the campaign for nuclear disarmament.

My wife and I became 'potteries' people on 2 September 1960. Our move to Stoke-on-Trent was necessitated by Bill Tudor's decision that I needed to become more conversant with the industries within North Staffordshire, for our members came from every conceivable industry, from the iron and steel works to gas and coke companies.

Stoke was in those days often described as a town of fire: it seemed that coal fuelled everything, from the gas works to the potteries. I shall never forget the bottle ovens at the potteries belching away, day in, day out, or the dense smoke that drifted from the chimneys of thousands of houses.

By this time, I had become more deeply involved in the electricity supply industry, representing our members employed in area boards and power stations on the joint industrial councils in both the West and East Midlands.

Recruiting new members was vital, and I well remember standing outside a wooden shed, in the middle of a field at Rugeley, Staffordshire, where a new power station was to be built. The only other people on site were the superintendent and a labourer who seemed to spend his time digging holes and making tea. I persuaded the labourer to sign a form to join the union and try to get new starters to do likewise. Initially he was reluctant, but my powers of persuasion seemed to overcome his reluctance and it was the start of a new branch of the union.

The electrical supply industry had a sort of magnetic hold over me, probably because of my electrical background. On the advice of others, however, I tended not to let on that I knew anything about electricity.

'Ask daft questions, let 'em think you know now't,' I had been told by a colleague. 'You'll be surprised at their reaction; they tell you twice as much, it's as though they take pity on you.'

One summer morning in 1965 I was called from a meeting at Electricity Board Headquarters at Halesowen, Worcestershire, to be told of the death of Reggie Parker, my friend and colleague of many years and the District Secretary of the Midlands area of the NUEFMEW. With mixed emotions I received official notification, from the Executive, that I would be the District Secretary as from 7 July 1965.

The promotion brought with it new responsibility. Previously, as assistant, I had only attended executive meetings in Transport House on occasions of special importance. Now, my attendance was required at all meetings; although we had no vote, each district secretary would be questioned as to his stewardship and have to give up-to-date reports on developments and negotiations within the industries in their respective districts.

It was a two-way forum for exchanging information and ideas and had the added bonus of enabling you to make your mark in the union, gain respect and sometimes even receive the odd pat on the back from other members.

I gained some prominence in the union when I successfully avoided a strike in the steel industry by pursuing arbitration. Little did I know how much this episode would help me on my way up the union ladder.

Then, for a short time, I was made a magistrate for Stoke-on-Trent. The office was not to last long, however, for it was announced at the next meeting of the Executive of the NUEFMEW that our General Secretary, Bill Tudor, had decided to retire at sixty. An election procedure would have to be decided and implemented as soon as possible, giving a short period of overlap between the General Secretary and the General Secretary elect.

Many other aspects relating to the future of the union had also to be considered, in particular that of the depletion of those funds which enabled the NUEFMEW to continue functioning as an autonomous body, separately registered as a trade union. It was hoped by the TGWU that the NUEFMEW would simply merge into the trade groups of the larger union, for there was strong feeling within the TUC at the time that it should reduce its total number of unions, either by transfer of engagements, straight amalgamation or other methods. They hoped that, by so doing, friction in industry would be reduced and industrial unions formed.

They had, however, misjudged how much this little union valued its autonomy, and they certainly did not think that it would dare to hold such different views from those of its big brother. Our Executive lay members made no bones about the fact that, rather than merging with the TGWU now, they would prefer to discuss the matter with other unions.

I was fully aware that this would be the first problem to be overcome by the new General Secretary, and with the electoral procedures decided upon, it was whispered that I was a likely candidate for the job. All of the factors were put on the scales, and I decided that the challenge of change weighed in favour of accepting nomination. There were three other nominations, all officers of the union, but I was the only one with mining experience.

I shall never forget Father, white-faced, lips trembling and near to tears, announcing one lunchtime: 'You've been elected General Secretary. The London office has just phoned and given me the message downstairs.'

I started work in the office in Transport House on 19 October 1966. I left Doris in Stoke and lived a lonely week in numerous London hotels, returning home sometimes only for a day at the weekend. Subsequent analysis of the election results showed that, in addition to securing the mining membership vote and much of the vote in the electricity supply industry, I had also received a large vote in the steel industry. I now had the responsibilities of the total union, and had to represent my members on various committees, including the National Industrial Councils in electricity supply, the Confederation of Shipbuilding and Engineering, and, perhaps most important of all, the Executive of the NUM.

Now there was the future of the NUEFMEW to deal with before the triennial conference of the union which was to be held in May 1967. My predecessor, Bill Tudor, had already paved the way for discussions with the Electrical Trades Union. The ETU had indicated quite clearly their desire to take over the NUEFMEW, thereby increasing their membership in the electricity supply industry and also, perhaps more crucial still, giving them an entrée to the mining industry and a seat on the NUM Executive. We had frank and amenable discussions with officers from the ETU like Frank Chapple and Les Cannon but, as General Secretary elect, I had unreservedly stated that I saw no possibility of such a merger occurring. There was, I suppose, a large degree of self-interest in my attitude, and justifiably I felt: after all, I had just receiving the voting confidence of my mining membership as well as that of the electricity supply industry. If anyone was to represent the mining members, then it had to be me: and, if possible, in an autonomous setting.

Abandoning that idea, and convincing the others that what we had once seen as a promising avenue was in fact a cul-de-sac, I decided to seek a meeting with Jack Jones, who was then the assistant executive secretary at the TGWU. He agreed to see me and was accompanied by the man who later became General Secretary of the TUC, Norman Willis.

I laid out the circumstances of the union, and asked what was on offer from the TGWU if we contemplated a revision of the amalgamation terms as laid down in the 1923 Agreement. As I suspected, the terms were documented and precise, though subject to discussion and negotiation, but far from acceptable.

Where to now? The only possibility was the NUM so I phoned Bill Paynter, the Secretary, at NUM headquarters, 222 Euston Road, London and explained the situation. He made it clear that the NUM would not tolerate any loss of membership or other unions becoming involved in the new arrangement. The issue was becoming even more complex, but a date was fixed for a meeting with our full Executive.

The day for the meeting drew nigh, and I was met by Sidney Ford, President of the NUM, sitting in his presidential chair with Bill Paynter on one side and Don Loney, Chief Executive Officer, on the other.

'Well, Roy,' said Sidney, 'we have already raised this question with our Executive, and we see no reason why the NUEF-MEW shouldn't become a constituent association of the NUM.'

My own Executive members and officers were, I felt, most pleased with the news, especially the lay members who had admired the colourful red leather armchairs in the room reserved for meetings of the NUM Executive, with its large semi-circular window, engraved with everyday scenes of working miners, pick-axes and shovels held aloft.

My earliest picture. It was taken outside Battram Primary School, Leicestershire, in 1929. I was five years old

Below: I spent my teenage years in one of these terraced cottages in Forty Row, Station Road, Bagworth. They were known as 'Forty Row' because there were forty cottages in all. We lived in the eleventh one up and Father kept a pig in the back garden. Pit towers and slag heaps dominate the landscape

'The beautiful one': my wife Doris during our courting days. The daughter of a miner, she always gave me loyal support

Below: Craftsmen always try to look smart. We put our jackets on over our overalls for this 1948 photograph outside the NCB's Mines' Mechanization Training Centre in Sheffield. That handsome young man on the far right is me. Note the tie-pin and slicked-back hair

There were, of course, many aspects to discuss, but none which they felt would cause difficulty. For instance, as a constituent association of the NUM, the 'area', as it is called (it can be a geographical or professional area), would be responsible for all its own administration, subject to the national rule book; it would be separately registered as a trade union; all officers at present receiving salaries would go on receiving them; and cars would be provided from the area funds. It would have its own executive committee, hold its own conferences to determine policy and, according to numerical strength, have representation on the NUM Executive. All areas have at least one Executive member, and some have two or three. As a result there are twenty-three Executive members, plus the President, the Secretary and Vice-President making a grand total of twenty-six. The Vice-President, like all Executive members, is elected every two years. The Secretary has no vote.

The NUM had quickly, and in a businesslike way, demonstrated their readiness to resolve the present difficulties, even if it were partly to ensure that other unions would not enter their own sphere of activity. I quickly analysed the proposals made by Sidney Ford, and weighed up the expense and implications of moving to London.

I reasoned that if the NUM were prepared to take over the whole of the NUEFMEW, why could they not just take over the mining membership? If their proposals were viable, why shouldn't they be valid for a smaller unit, more economically staffed? If such a position was negotiable, why should I live in the South of England, while membership was mainly in the Midlands and the North? Would it not be better, given my experience, if I were to act solely for the mining craftsmen? Wasn't it they who had started me on my career? Equally, weren't the other officers in the union better equipped to represent their individual industrial branches?

I put all this to the NUM and got an affirmative reply to my suggestions. So, by the time of our own Executive meeting, the seeds of change had been sown. This meeting was not a happy one for the proposed changes provoked reactions which, it seemed to me, bordered on the irrational or the ridiculous.

Nevertheless, when the meeting was declared closed, the matter was resolved. I had been fascinated by the way that gentle understanding and persuasion had worked so successfully.

Conference-time in May seemed to come early that year of 1967, and I was filled with a great feeling of trepidation as Doris and I journeyed to Great Yarmouth for what was to be my first conference as General Secretary of the NUEFMEW and the last for the union in its present form.

I had carefully written my speech to conference during many hours alone at night in my hotel bedroom in London. I was going to cover the economic position, expenditure on benefits, the 1923 Agreement and, most important of all, the fact that the union would cease to function as from 30 July, the mining members forming a constituent association of the NUM and the rest of the membership being absorbed into the respective trade groups in the TGWU.

'Roy,' said Jack Jones, who had been invited to talk to delegates, as we sat down to dinner the night before conference began, 'if you pull this off, I'm going to buy you the biggest glass of beer you've ever had.'

The following day I made my speech, which lasted for an hour and a half. There were many questions to be answered, and it seemed that delegates were just as sad as Executive members at the impending loss of their own union. But, when the vote was taken, there was only one dissentient – a young man from the President's branch who, we found out later, had been specially briefed by the President. The whole thing had gone without a hitch and I notified the NUM straightaway.

The following weeks were spent dealing with officers' and staff problems, finances and all other issues necessary to ensure the change went smoothly. Having declined an offer to remain within the TGWU as Power Group/Trade Group National Officer, I sank my future with the NUM. I moved back to Stoke-on-Trent and was delighted to be with Doris again. I also resumed magisterial duties.

I was doing a daily journey of thirty-six miles to the office in Stafford. But now, I had a car instead of a bike. We had had to borrow £5,000 from the NUM to purchase two cars – one for my colleague, Michael Carey, and one for me. We only had £5,000 in the new area funds, which had been transferred from the old union.

With benefits to members remaining as before, all contributions were quickly being reimbursed back to the members. At this rate, the new area would not survive for long. If subsidization were sought from the NUM, they were bound to suggest merging with the other miners' areas with which our membership overlapped, and this might well lead to our autonomy being lessened. If we were to project the aspirations of the craftsmen, we had to keep our seat on the NUM Executive. So we had somehow to improve financial reserves and the quickest way seemed to be by scrapping the benefits which were depleting the funds. This in itself would not be easy, but motivating members to do it turned out to be simpler, though there was a nail-biting half-hour before we did so.

The Inaugural Conference was held at the Grand Hotel, Hanley, Stoke-on-Trent on 8 and 9 April 1968. The constitution and rule book had been drawn up, based largely on the model rules of the NUM and our former union. Speakers from the NUM and the NCB had been invited. This was a make or break conference for me: I knew that if members did not make the right decisions as far as I was concerned, I would be out of a job and would be better off going back to the pit.

The first day was a day of tolerant debate. It was not until the next day that we reached the crucial resolution that the membership should be merged with other NUM areas, thus spelling the end for the Power Group. I moved it on behalf of our Executive and the motion was seconded. The first person, however, to march to the rostrum to enter the debate was my brother John, a delegate from Ellistown Colliery, Leicestershire. Most are sure to say I fixed it. I know I hadn't, and the look on his face – one of grim determination – was enough to prove the others wrong. The message was simple: 'Mr President, Delegates – brother: if that is the best you can do for us, find yourself another job.' He stalked back to his seat leaving the way clear for others to go up to the rostrum. It was exhilarating. I had a union.

Then I proposed the resolution to scrap sickness benefits. Now, however, subsequent speakers were so forceful in their attacks that my feeling of exhilaration turned to dismay. Miracles apart, it seemed obvious that a majority would vote against the proposal.

'Right to reply,' I said, and went up to the rostrum. 'Today you have concluded that you want to remain an autonomous body, able to act in the interest of those you represent. Nobody has suggested that contributions should be increased to a higher level than that paid by the miners so as to be able to keep the sickness benefits. You are all intelligent men, as economically aware as me. It is no use setting me an impossible task. I am now going to lead your Executive Committee out of the hall and whilst we are out, you had better decide whether you want a union or not.'

I didn't know whether the Executive members would follow, but they did. Half an hour elapsed, the local Pressmen wondering what on earth was happening as they stood with us at the top of the staircase.

We were called back in and told that they had agreed to accept, unanimously. We could now start to build the Power Group of the NUM into what we wished it to be: a force for the advancement of miners' aspirations. I was delighted and relieved.

– 2 –

The Gormley Era

The industry was now in what I see as the years of consolidation. By the late 1960s consultation and conciliation procedures had developed to an unprecedented high level, while the NCB's educational programme, the 'Ladder Plan', had enabled many in the industry to advance their status. It really was possible now to go from being pit lad to Chairman of the Board. The dream many people had nurtured on nationalization day of taking over the industry was beginning to become a reality.

Nevertheless, we were also experiencing a period of paternalism, ably generated and implemented by the NCB Chairman at that time, Alf Robens. There were many, many pit closures, and the mechanization of the remaining pits continued apace. There was also considerable reorganization of the administration, as well as the introduction of the National Power Loading Agreement which removed contract and piecework systems and replaced them with nationally agreed rates. Wage levels had not advanced as much as many had hoped, and surface workers, craftsmen included, were fast falling down the league table of earnings.

To a great degree it could be alleged that the NEC, of which I of course was now a member, had succumbed to this era of paternalism. It was a period of right-wing domination, almost a dictatorship, and we were expected to conform. Inevitably, though, a rebellion was brewing.

Deciding to let everyone know that the Power Group existed, we placed a resolution on the NUM annual conference agenda in 1969 calling for a merger of all craftsmen's groups. We subsequently arranged meetings of representatives of all craftsmen's groups. Almost immediately, the NUM President, Sidney Ford, called our action unconstitutional. My only support came from someone who was soon to make a name for himself: Joe Gormley, who was at that time the General Secretary for the Lancashire Miners. He told me he was 'all for splinter groups' and felt that they made life interesting.

Later in 1969 surface workers in Yorkshire started strike action. Our Power Group membership soon became involved and a decision was taken by our Executive to call a one-day strike. The day before the strike was to take place, the NCB conceded the full claim of the union – the first and only time they had ever done so. It was too late to call off the Power Group action, and it was years before we were forgiven.

This dispute was significant on two counts. Firstly, it was a complete victory for the union and, secondly, I became aware of a union activist in Yorkshire named Arthur Scargill. I remember seeing him on the television screen. He was pictured in a duffle coat on the pit surface, exhorting the men to action. Little did I think that this man would in 1984 be voted 'Man of the Year' by BBC Radio 4 listeners.

In 1969 Sidney Ford retired from the position of President of the NUM, and procedures started for the election of a successor. Joe Gormley had decided to run and, though I had mixed feelings about it, my own Power Group had decided to nominate me too. I remember Joe Gormley coming up to me and asking: 'Are you definitely running, Roy? You know it will split the right-wing vote and let McGahey in.'

He was referring to Mick McGahey, the Communist President of the Scottish area. It was generally recognized that he was a man of great ability, who was particularly impressive when speaking at Conferences, cleverly manipulating his listeners' emotions. Yet we suspected that he might be a man prepared to use any tactics to achieve his aims.

'Not if you withdraw it won't, Joe,' I had replied. But I sensed there was no chance of that, for I knew full well that Joe was an ambitious and determined man.

I pondered on my chances and decided they were not really

very good. Despite my years in the industry, I was a craftsman, and the NUM and the NCB had always considered craftsmen as necessary evils – especially my own group with our long-standing association with the TGWU. Then a letter arrived from Nicholas Ridley, Secretary of State for Energy, asking me to see him about becoming a part-time Board Member of the Midlands Electricity Board. I duly decided not to run for presidency and became a part-time member of the Board.

I have never regretted my decision. Joe Gormley became President of the NUM on 10 June 1971. Mick McGahey became Vice-President the same year. The Gormley era was a good one for the miners. Joe was a man determined not to be deflected from his aim of improving the lot of all miners. He was a pragmatic realist and a democrat, who appreciated that men went to work so as to provide the best for their families. He was also a hard negotiator, as we were to see in the months that followed.

The industrial unrest, as seen in 1969, far from subsiding in the next two years, kept on bubbling almost continuously. The unions were not happy and the delegates made no secret of the fact at the NUM 1971 Annual Conference. The answer of the NCB to the wage claim that year was totally unsatisfactory. The individual ballot vote of the members was held, and resulted in a majority voting in favour of the NUM Executive calling strike action. I had no compunction about saying to Joe: 'That's it then – it's time to strike.' The date was decided, the strike called and started.

Little was left to chance; every aspect was fully debated and controlled at a national level, from programmes for picketing to detailing information on benefit entitlements and updating as the weeks went by. Demonstrations and lobbies of Parliament showed that public support was running high; trade union solidarity was magnificent. Everyone seemed to recognize that the miners were justified in their fight for better wages and conditions.

Much has been written, much has been claimed and much has been said about the 1972 strike.

Immediately the strike started, our offices in Stafford

became the control centre. From here, with military precision, pickets were organized and deployed far afield to power stations everywhere, including the south coast. Here too we dealt with the problems of shelter, food, and clothing as well as the non-picketing miners' individual problems. Yet, in sharp contrast to the 1984-5 strike, it was also very peaceful. We managed to keep on good terms with the police; in fact, many of them were presented with miners' lamps as a token of gratitude at the end of the strike.

One of the most memorable episodes of the strike was the picketing of Saltley Gas Works in the Midlands. Token picketing at Saltley had failed to stop a mountain of coal building up at the gas works and a continuous stream of lorries entering and leaving. Obviously action needed to be stepped up. So the next day, I and a colleague met the chief of police in Birmingham and told him frankly of our intentions to try and organize mass-picketing. Our intention was not to be violent, but rather to demonstrate how many people there were who strongly supported the miners' cause.

By lunchtime the following day we had large numbers of pickets, all in need of food, so my colleague, Michael Carey, and I got in the car and headed for the nearest Co-op store. We explained our predicament to the manager. He suggested giving them bread and cheese, and put two large cheeses on the counter. I drove back, the back seat full of sliced bread and the front full of cheese. We arrived at the works, slapped the cheese between slices of bread, and served the queuing men through the car window.

Feeding the men on a Sunday was more difficult, for with most shops shut we had to drive around the back streets seeking a corner store. Eventually we found a small shop, run by a Pakistani and his wife, and a shelf full of boxes of Dairylea cheese. 'We'll take all those,' I said, 'and all those loaves of bread stacked in the corner. Give us those bunches of bananas as well and we'll take all those bottles of milk on the floor!'

We left the Pakistani lady wide-eyed with amazement, and her husband trembling with excitement. As we drove off, we heard him shout; 'Come back tomorrow, Sahib!'

But we still needed more pickets and more food. Miners'
wives arrived with wash-boilers filled with hot soup and the
TGWU organized deliveries of meat pies, though I regret to say
some ended up being thrown at lorries as miners became
increasingly frustrated.

We had extra support from miners in Wales and Yorkshire,
and with the Scottish miners there even came a piper in full
regalia. The contingent from Yorkshire included the man I had
briefly seen on television: Arthur Scargill. He stood beside me
in a telephone box while I implored the Yorkshire area General
Secretary, Sidney Schofield, to send more pickets.

A meeting of the NUM Executive had been called for Thursday. During the meeting we heard that Saltley Gas Works had
closed due to the picketing, an event which Arthur Scargill has
since held up as an example of what can be achieved by the solidarity of the working classes. The atmosphere in the meeting
was tense as each of us read the content of the award decided
upon by the Wilberforce Inquiry. This was an inquiry set up by
the Conservative Government in 1972 with the specific aim of
resolving the dispute.

I was not impressed by the offer; certainly not after the weeks
of misery we had endured. The award still did not remove the
anomalies for craftsmen, particularly the five-day week bonus.
I had always considered this a pernicious agreement for it
meant that some men, particularly craftsmen, who were
obliged to work at weekends, would lose two days' pay if they
had the temerity to take Monday off for a rest.

There was some discussion, and Joe Gormley quickly decided
to put the matter to the vote. He miscalculated the mood, I
thought, because he expected acceptance, but the majority
voted against, myself included. 'You've voted with the Com-
mies,' I was later told.

Joe intervened in the discussion. 'Right, let's decide on what
we do want then. What will we settle for?' The trouble was that
everybody wanted something different.

That evening the NUM Executive transferred to a room in 10
Downing Street, and Joe and the other officials had talks with
the Prime Minister, Ted Heath. The night was a long one, with

Joe and the officials marching between the downstairs room we had been given and the room upstairs in which they were meeting Ted Heath. We sat there all evening in a large, sparsely furnished room, watching at hourly intervals the news on television. We watched anxiously as we saw angry area officials demanding to know what we were playing at. I think they thought we were living it up in Downing Street. The truth was that we were getting tired and hungry. We finally asked Downing Street staff if we could have something to eat. One of them retorted: 'It's not a canteen here, you know!' but we did get some beer and some rather tired-looking sandwiches, curling up at the edges.

The tension mounted each time Joe came back to us. We still refused to settle. 'Get the abolition of the five-day week bonus, Joe,' I said, as he turned to go up the stairs yet again, 'and then I will propose that we settle.' It was a tough nut to crack but, after what seemed like hours, Joe returned, announcing success.

By the time the NUM Conference came around in 1973, the Heath Government was still in power, economic problems persisted, inflation needed to be curbed, and statutory wage control had been introduced. All of this served to encourage the miners to go higher up the wages league table again. Their success of 1972 had led many miners to believe that they were invincible.

Once again a ballot vote resulted in the NUM Executive being given the right to call strike action. This time, however, the majority in favour was smaller.

A ban on overtime was introduced in November. The strike of 1972 had taught us to implement procedures, and there was also full co-operation from the unions in the TUC.

Now that we had picketing techniques down to a fine art and the support of other unions behind us, electricity supplies were soon affected. We eventually arrived at a point where much of the industry was only able to operate intermittently and this resulted in the statutory introduction in January 1974 of a three-day week.

Solidarity among the miners and other trade unions was as strong as ever, but it was apparent that the adversities faced by the general public as a result of power-cuts were generating a tenacity and determination unseen since the war.

Workers were ingeniously devising methods of getting to work and, having got there, were trying to maintain normal production levels over the three permitted days. They hoped thus to conserve supplies to industries.

As the situation in the country reached crisis proportions, the whole of the NUM Executive found themselves yet again in 10 Downing Street, this time meeting Ted Heath with other members of the Cabinet, such as William Whitelaw and Peter Walker.

We were invited to lunch in Downing Street, and the meal was followed by a meeting. Despite the circumstances, I found Ted Heath to be easy-going and good company. I remember enjoying a scotch and dry with him before lunch, and, in our efforts I suppose to try to think of a non-political topic of conversation, we came round to the question of personal security. We asked him whether he ever worried for his life. He replied that, of course, he had thought about the risks, but accepted them as being part of his job. He told us, laughing, how he was always trying to pick new routes when he walked to the House of Commons.

At lunch I found myself sitting next to Maurice Macmillan, and we got talking about his father, Harold. I was reminded of this occasion when in the autumn of 1984 Harold Macmillan, now the Earl of Stockton, spoke so feelingly in the House of Lords about the present plight of miners and their families.

After lunch came the meeting. Joe Gormley was, I sensed, ready to settle for the proposed offer. I remember Willie Whitelaw imploring us to settle for the terms being offered. I am sure he believed that all that was needed was a burst of fatherly discourse to end the dispute. As we filed out of the meeting room, Ted Heath and Peter Walker stood together watching us go out. One of them asked as I went past, 'What are our chances, Mr Ottey?' I did not hesitate to advise them to 'stick', meaning that I thought the offer would be accepted.

Afterwards, the NUM Executive met and argued the pros and cons of the position we were in, and Joe took the vote. Only five of us voted to accept: the majority were in favour of continuing the struggle. The strike started on 9 February 1974.

I shall never forget the tear that slid down Joe's face as we walked towards the door, and out into the falling snowflakes, to meet the ever-present journalists. Even now, I find it hard to believe that in February 1974 the miners brought down the Heath Government: for the Prime Minister decided to go to the country, and the people decided, admittedly only by a hairbreadth, that there should be a change of government. As a result of the miners' claims being settled by the incoming Labour Government, I feel that the following years produced an inflationary spiral by leap-frogging wage claims from which the economy has not yet recovered.

The following years, in which we pursued international co-operation with miners' unions all over the world, gave me a marvellous opportunity to view different cultures: I visited India, Moscow, Siberia, the Ukraine, East Germany, China, Hungary, West Germany, Sweden and Spain.

But there was also sadness in store for me when in 1974 my colleague Michael Carey, who had been for some time suffering from a heart condition, died suddenly at only fifty years of age. Circumstances dictated that there would be no replacement officer. I would be the only elected official, Executive members assisting where possible and if necessary.

As the years went by the divide between the left and the right of the NUM Executive seemed to become more marked. Perhaps this had something to do with the arrival on the Executive of Arthur Scargill, who had risen quickly from being Compensation Officer for the Yorkshire area, claiming money from the NCB for accidents resulting from negligence, to President of that area. I began to feel that the left were enjoying power without responsibility, for, though much was being achieved, both for the miners and the industry, the left rarely voted for any of the achievements. Arthur himself, it seemed, voted *for* hardly anything; he always seemed to vote against. Of course, this put him in the enviable position of being able to leave meetings and announce to all that, if the Executive had listened to him, they would have gained an even greater prize.

As it was, the prizes were not bad: miners now had workwear provided for them – previously it had been provided by the men themselves; there was an all-embracing scheme for the widows and victims of pneumoconiosis – dust disease; there was earlier non-compulsory retirement with increased money; and there was an incentive bonus scheme. The latter was vociferously and antagonistically opposed by the left, but it was gradually introduced area by area and finally the left-wing areas were forced by their members to accept the scheme. Average earnings in the industry were now at the top of the league: with incentives and overtime, some miners could now earn up to £10,000 a year.

Of course, there was still room for improvement. There always is, especially in the mining industry. Men can graduate to the coal-face and enjoy the highest paid jobs only to find themselves faced with taking a drop in salary if for any reason, perhaps through injury or illness, they are unable to continue at the coal-face. To this day this issue has not been resolved.

One thing I have always admired about the left is their unswerving dedication to the cause. Yet the concepts of negotiation and compromise seemed to be alien to them. Resolutions to Annual Conference would always carry the threat of industrial action. Fortunately, the miners themselves knew that there was always a 'safety valve': the individual ballot vote.

Such was the situation when, outraged and incensed by the excessive demands and threats of action, Joe Gormley started to talk about retiring early. But he was obviously concerned about what would happen to the union if he did, for by continuing until he was sixty-five, he effectively ensured that the Vice-President, the Communist from Scotland, Mick McGahey, would never succeed him, for Mick had by then reached the age of fifty-five and was unable to run for the job in accordance with the rules, which state that no one over that age is eligible for election.

We now looked around for a candidate to succeed Joe. It was obvious that Arthur Scargill would be the left-wing candidate, but who would it be for the right?

The right wing met at Joe's home one evening to consider the possibilities. There was certainly not going to be one runner only: we were so divided. I thought it should be Trevor Bell, who had taken over from Les Storey as the Colliery Officials and Staffs' area representative on the Executive. Two others volunteered: Ray Chadburn, President of the Nottinghamshire area, and Denis Murphy, President of the Northumberland area. I remember Denis, his eyes twinkling, saying, 'I can run, you know. There's no qualifications needed for this job, y'know. I only have to get the votes.'

In the end Denis didn't run, leaving Trevor Bell, Ray Chadburn and Bernard Donaghy, President of the Lancashire miners, to fight it out with Arthur Scargill. Although they certainly gave him a run for his money, the almost incessant projections in the media, which loved focusing on Arthur, served to ensure that in December 1981 Arthur became President of the NUM for life, achieving a victory unsurpassed by any predecessor: 70.3 per cent of the membership had backed his presidency. No one could say that he hadn't worked for it: he is one of the hardest workers I have ever known.

Through his presidential campaign Arthur Scargill had chosen pit closures as the main issue upon which it was felt the membership should focus their attention. He wanted to galvanize the miners into action, by which I mean industrial action, to secure the establishment of a socialist society in Britain. It seemed clear to me that this was not necessarily what the miners themselves desired.

Arthur had good grounds for presuming that members would react positively to his exhortations. For earlier in the year, on 10 February 1981, when the Chairman of the NCB, Derek Ezra, announced a plan which would include the closure of up to fifty pits with the loss of about 30,000 jobs in the industry, there was immediate strike action by South Wales and Kent areas, supported by Scotland, Durham and Yorkshire, with the threat of national action by 23 February. As a result, the Government and the NCB withdrew the plan.

'Pit closures will only be stopped if there is a determination on the part of our membership to resist any further rape of our industry and insist that no pits should be closed unless on the ground of proven exhaustion,' said Arthur in his campaign document 'Miners in the 80s'. He went on to speak of the 'lack of democracy' within the union:

It is because of the unrepresentative nature of the NEC who ignore decisions of the annual conference and in many cases actively oppose those democratic decisions. The answer is to introduce the same voting structure within the NEC as already applies in the National Conference. Real democracy will only come about when that kind of system is introduced so that ordinary members can feel confident that their involvement in the union and their commitment to its purpose will be reflected directly in policy decisions.

I considered such statements as these a real effrontery to members; he seemed to be completely ignoring the fact that almost every important decision affecting the members had been the subject of an individual ballot vote. If that wasn't real democracy, then what was?

The extent to which our chances of obtaining future democracy were jeopardized was to be starkly demonstrated at a Special Delegate Conference on Friday, 18 December 1981. The annual wages claim had reached final negotiations, and the conference was called to debate the final offer. Joe Gormley, who was still acting President, was unable to be present and the Vice-President, Mick McGahey, took the chair.

The morning was freezing cold, and delegates arriving at Congress Hall, TUC headquarters, were met by a large number of lobbyists outside, who were no doubt paid to be present by militants from some areas.

Opening the proceedings, Mick McGahey proposed that the lobbyists should be allowed into the Conference, although they were not to take part in the proceedings. The Press was present and this in itself provided precedent, he said.

The proposition was agreed by Conference delegates and the lobbyists came in, outnumbering the delegates by about five to one. The whole thing had obviously been carefully calculated: to have expected that such a situation would not have any effect on delegates present would have been too naive for words. In fact, the inevitable effect was that lobbyists hissed speakers with whom they disagreed, and delegates admitted afterwards that they had felt intimidated by the hostile atmosphere.

Conference decided to reject the NCB offer and recommend rejection of the offer to the membership in a ballot vote for strike action.

I was troubled with doubts for the future, and convinced that the members of the union were to become secondary and subjugated to the interest of achieving the political desires of the newly-elected President and his supporters. So I decided to send a Christmas message to the members of my branches. It was published by the local paper, the *Evening Sentinel*, and a copy of the letter was sent to Arthur Scargill.

21 December 1981

Dear Colleagues,

Over the weekend, away from the emotive atmosphere of the Special Delegate Conference, I have constantly reflected upon the utterances of the President Elect, Mr Arthur Scargill. Many of you will have seen and heard them on television.

I refer particularly to the statement that 'miners should be told that a vote against the recommendation of Conference will be a betrayal of the union'.

My dictionary states: 'Betrayal: the act of betraying; a breach of trust or confidence; a deceitful act'.

Throughout the negotiations I have ensured that you have had the opportunity of presenting to the members the whole of the documentation that has been available to the negotiators.

My purpose in doing so has always been the recognition that each of our members is equally as intelligent, if not more so, than myself or any other person who has the privilege of representing them.

The purpose of our predecessors enshrining in the rules that a secret individual ballot vote be taken before National Strike action takes place was to give the supreme decision to those who are 'the Union'.

For Mr Scargill to say, therefore, that miners who vote against his opinion are betrayers of the union is, in my opinion, akin to the attitudes of the Polish Government and the extremist Governments of Latin America and elsewhere.

I have little doubt but that Power Group members will exercise their vote in the forthcoming ballot democratically and without regard to other than their own self-determined analysis of the information available to them in our free Society.

That is their right, but it is obvious that there are some who think they are more intelligent and should have the right to instruct us all.

We shall need to be constantly vigilant against surrendering our individual ballot vote arising from the intimidatory methods of the real deceivers.

May I take this opportunity, in my final communication to you of the year, to thank you for the work and loyalty you have given over the past 12 months and ask you to convey to all members and their families my sincere wishes for a Happy Christmas and a Good New Year.

Yours sincerely,
J.R. Ottey
General Secretary

P.S. Copy to Mr A. Scargill

The day before the ballot, Joe Gormley made a full-page statement in the *Daily Express* which, whilst not categorically telling the membership which way to vote, certainly advised them as to which way Joe would vote.

A majority of the members – 55 per cent – voted to accept and all hell was let loose at the next NUM Executive meeting, the left moving a vote of censure on Joe and some members of the Executive nearly coming to blows. We narrowly defeated the censure motion by 13 votes to 12.

There was comfort in having won the vote, but the decision gave little hope for the future. The final few weeks were not to be happy ones for Joe but I am sure he was content that the members had again backed his judgement.

The last NUM Executive meeting to be held in Joe's presence took place in Cumbria. It was an important meeting for me too, for on the agenda was an item relating to my own pension. A motion was carried which restored just over half the loss I had suffered in the transition from one union to the other in 1967. For this I was indebted to Mick McGahey.

Sitting next to him at the TUC Annual Conference in September 1981 and listening to a TGWU delegate lambasting the Government about low pension rates, I had muttered to myself, 'And the unions are as bad.'

'What do you mean?' asked Mick abruptly.

I told him about my predicament and he was so intrigued

that I promised to let him have my personal file on the subject. He subsequently returned it, slapping it down on a table and exclaiming, 'I think it's diabolical how you have been treated! Write to Lawrence Daly [then the General Secretary] and tell him you want a meeting with him, Gormley and me.'

That meeting was not necessary; Mick's word was sufficient. I shook his hand in appreciation after the Executive meeting, but was filled with a mixture of sadness and apprehension as Joe walked away for the last time.

Joe Gormley was not only a level-headed negotiator, believing in compromise rather than constant confrontation, but also an internationalist, who fostered an almost unshatterable belief that miners were miners wherever they lived, no matter the country or the ideological circumstances. He firmly believed that the NUM, which was renowned for its democratic values, had a duty to assist, advise, listen to and learn from miners' unions all over the world.

Joe Gormley's whole attitude was to be summed up years later when I had arranged, shortly before his retirement, for him to address a large gathering of members of the British Institute of Management at the North Stafford Hotel, Stoke-on-Trent, in 1981. The organizers had suggested that the theme for his address be entitled 'The role of the trade unions in the '80s'.

'I've got no brief, Roy. What am I going to say to them?' he asked while we had a drink at the hotel bar. 'You'll tell them something, Joe,' I replied.

Introduced by the Chairman, Joe said simply: 'The role of the trade union in the '80s is the same as it has always been. First, to sit down with management and decide together how to create the wealth. Second, to sit down again with management and decide how best to share it out. Now that's the end of the story. What questions do you want to ask me?'

He had the audience sitting in the palm of his hand and he loved the challenge of the crowd. A lifelong member of the Labour Party, he was a democrat to the last.

He was also a very good friend. Doris and I had many enjoyable times with Joe and his wife Nellie. We often went out with

them during conferences and once stayed at their home in Sun-
bury-on-Thames. Joe simply thrived on company.

A generous man, one of his greatest pleasures was good food
and wine; he was something of a gourmet. 'Get it down yer, lad,'
he chuckled after I had been served the biggest T-bone steak I
had ever seen in my life. He isn't a lot older than me, but always
calls me 'lad'.

He was a great lover of fun, and particularly enjoyed a good
old sing-song at conference reunions. Next to Sid Vincent, he
had the best singing voice on the NUM Executive.

But he also had tremendous integrity: he often told those
who aspired after his job – including Arthur Scargill – 'The
buck stops here', pointing to himself. I admired him for never
trying to wriggle out of a situation by blaming the members.

On 24 June 1982 I witnessed my first confrontation between
Arthur Scargill and the NCB. A joint review meeting had
taken place in May, and this was a sort of follow-up meeting
between the NUM Executive and the NCB. It was chaired by
Norman Siddall. He had now become NCB Chairman, after a
lifetime spent in the industry, during which time he had risen
from pit lad to Chairman. In fact, Norman's meteoric rise was
precisely the sort of thing we had anticipated when the industry was nationalized.

We went to Hobart House, NCB headquarters in Grosvenor
Place, London. We took our places around the tables in our
usual room – Room 16. The curtains were drawn, as normal,
and in the vast mirror at one end we could see the backs of the
NCB officials. Arthur Scargill, sitting opposite Norman Siddall, referred to discussion which had taken place at the previous joint review meeting, and indicated that the NCB had
given an assurance that full information would be provided on
pit closures within the industry.

He went on to say that the brief produced by the NCB did not
provide the information. Was the Chairman prepared to make
the facts available?

I couldn't help recalling that in February 1981 the NCB had
indeed provided a so-called 'hit list' – the list of mines
threatened by closure – but that the union had vociferously

objected to it and had succeeded in getting it removed. However, Arthur Scargill repeated the question. Norman Siddall replied that the NCB did not have a list of potential closures: the NCB document made it clear that it was inappropriate to speculate at national level on future closures. In the NCB's view these should be identified at local level and the appropriate arrangements made for the transfer of men. There had to be discussion between all parties involved.

Arthur Scargill stated that the NCB had been warned that the list would be required, and the Deputy Chairman, James Cowan, said: 'I have tried to tell Mr Scargill that we haven't got a list. I have mentioned Killock pit [Scotland] where, despite results, we have used technology and all other means to keep it open. How can we provide a list when we are doing this? No matter what political argument Mr Scargill might have, we have no list.'

Arthur Scargill retaliated by pointing out that there had been eight or nine closures in the last year and said the NCB knew where the pits were but had refused to say so.

James Cowan retorted: 'What would you want to do with the list?'

Several of the union's Executive members commented that this would be a question for the NEC to decide. They then prepared to leave, rising from their seats with their briefcases, and marched out of the room.

However, I stayed behind and insisted on asking questions on behalf of the Power Group. At this stage I then informed Norman Siddall that I knew of two pits in Staffordshire, through the review procedure,* that were due to close; surely the NCB would provide a list of other pits in other areas which were also closing? He replied that he would do this. Arthur was not at all pleased with me, but I felt that this was the only list the NCB could provide.

I was incensed by Arthur's behaviour at this meeting: here

---

* This is a system whereby all collieries are jointly reviewed by the NUM and the NCB about every three months from the point of view of productivity and finance.

he was demanding a list at a national level, instead of accepting the Chairman's invitation to sit down, with the NCB and the unions, and discuss the problems of the industry as we had since the earliest days of nationalization. The events of this meeting left me in no doubt that the aim within the NUM was to inflame the situation by rousing the passions of the membership.

In later years Arthur Scargill has turned full circle, insisting that if the NCB withdraws the list of closures he will be only too ready to sit down and discuss the future of the industry. I can only say that the invitation to do this was extended by Norman Siddall way back in June 1982, but that NUM leaders declined the offer, preferring to choose confrontation to consultation.

In the weeks that followed that episode, efforts were mainly channelled towards the forthcoming NUM Annual Conference, which is always held in the first full week in July. My wife, however, had to go into hospital for a serious operation the week before and, consequently, I missed the Conference for the first time ever.

Arthur and his wife Anne expressed their concern in a way that I will always remember. On an evening visit to the hospital I found nurses and patients chatting with excitement and bursting to tell me that *the* Arthur Scargill had sent a large bouquet of flowers to my wife. It was a great event, appreciated by all, and helped to relieve the traumatic tensions which had built up.

Arthur is a strange mixture of ruthlessness and sensitivity. He gives the impression of being an unfeeling 'tough guy', but his actions sometimes reveal another side to his character. 'The trouble is, you never listen to other people's points of view!' I once shouted at him when he was making some point or other. He looked at me with a hurt expression on his face, and I really thought he was going to burst into tears.

He also has an endearing self-deprecatory quality about him. 'You're looking smart, Arthur,' I once remarked when he appeared in an expensive-looking brown sports jacket. 'Oh, it's only one I got from the market!' he grinned.

Of course, I was disappointed at missing the first Conference of the NUM with Arthur Scargill at the helm. But my delegates did bring back a copy of Arthur's first presidential address which I read eagerly. No one can doubt Arthur's consistency.

He repeated much of what he had already outlined in his manifesto: namely, that he was not prepared to compromise his policies or 'prostitute . . . principles': that pits should not be closed unless exhausted; that leadership in the past had been inefficient; that the Conference was the supreme authority of the union and that 'no matter what judges have said or will say' Conference's decisions are sacrosanct; that he would not engage in 'secret' dealings; and that, if the union's claims could not be met through negotiation, then he would demand backing in an individual ballot.

He concluded:

> British miners will take industrial action whenever they consider it necessary: we will use whatever methods are considered appropriate: *we do not and will not* recognize distinctions between forms of picketing.

The next important event was the TUC Conference for, here again, we were to see the NUM Executive's intention to ignore the individual ballot vote of the NUM members. The Health Service unions were in dispute and the TUC had decided to call a day of action for 22 September.

Much to my surprise, I received a statement from NUM head office, stating that there had been a unanimous decision of the Executive to take strike action on 22 September in support of the Health Service unions. I, for one, had not been involved in any such decision.

My own Power Group Executive and many members were angry that they had not been consulted and asked to decide by ballot. We judged it best to delay our objection, however, until after the day of action so as not to affect the support the health workers were getting.

I failed to get a formal withdrawal of the circular at the next Executive meeting, and when we sought legal advice, the Power Group's view that the strike was contrary to union rules was confirmed. Subsequently, all Power Group members were advised that, henceforth, they should consider that strike action should never be taken unless an individual ballot vote had been held. After all, they were the members, and it was vital that they had the opportunity to take part in any decision-making which affected their livelihood and future. We would not sit idly by and accept dictatorship on any issue.

Negotiations with the NCB on the wages claim had started on 15 September. The package including a £115 minimum wage which was a 26 per cent average increase, the introduction of a four-day working week and retirement at fifty-five with lump sum payments equal to redundancy payments. Protection of earnings for men unable to continue in a high-paid job was also under discussion.

But a major talking-point was that in the wage demand was a call for an assurance from the NCB that there would be no more pit-, plant- or unit-closures (unless reserves were exhausted) and no further run-down in manpower, for, as we reminded them, 22,000 jobs had been lost in the previous eighteen months.

A Special NUM Conference decided on 4 October 1982 that both wages and pit closures should appear on a ballot paper which recommended that the members gave authority to the Executive to take industrial action. This brought an immediate reaction from many rank-and-file members in the coalfields who argued – and quite rightly in my opinion – that the two items should be dealt with separately and that the linking of the emotive question of pit closures with pay was just another attempt by the left wing within the NUM to bring about a strike.

On 17 October Arthur Scargill addressed Power Group delegates at a weekend school in Stoke-on-Trent, firstly telling them that the NUM did not have the money to provide strike pay and, that if the total assets of the union were divided amongst them, it would only amount to a one-off payment of £16.

'Throughout the history of the NUM,' he told delegates, 'the membership has taken action as an industrial unit. When it has been one man affected we have all been affected. It is not a weakness, it is a strength.'

Pressed about the two items on the ballot paper, he claimed that 11,000 jobs had been lost since April of that year and the NCB were pursuing a policy of pit closures by stealth. I presumed that Arthur was referring to the review procedure which had the full agreement of the union areas and under which all possible closures were fully discussed by all interested parties.

He went on: 'I will call a special Executive meeting to remove closures from the ballot paper if the NCB give an assurance that there will be no pits shut and no running down of manpower, except in the case of exhaustion of reserves.'

He said support for the overtime ban, introduced to give more strength to the miners' campaign, had grown, and the union was heading for victory. 'We can win a satisfactory settlement on wages provided we have the backing of the members. The Coal Board should be told to go to the Government to provide the cash to give miners their justified claims on wages, shorter working week and early retirement.'

This address was made on the eve of a series of rallies throughout the coalfields, so members throughout Britain heard the same message.

Yet the result of the ballot, announced at a special NUM Executive meeting on 2 November 1982, was a disaster as far as the left wing was concerned. Instead of the vote for strike action increasing from the last ballot, it had decreased, and of the 206,825 who had voted validly (i.e. 87 per cent of the membership) 125,233 (61 per cent) were against striking.

I commented in the Press: 'Once again Power Group members, with a vote of 85 per cent against strike, have demonstrated their ability to reflect the true views of the miners. The Power Group Executive have consistently opposed the overtime ban and the joining of pit closures and pay on the ballot paper. Acceptance of the pay offer has saved us from what could have been a lengthy strike which could have led to more pits closing.'

I was certain that if we had sat down and discussed the problems of the industry, we could have obtained better rewards for the members.

Not one to dwell on defeat, Arthur Scargill said at a press conference afterwards that the result of the pay ballot was disappointing, and went on to declare that the union had in their possession an NCB document which was 'top secret' and listed seventy-five pits for closure over the next five years. We were to hear more of it when on 24 January 1983 the NCB and the NUM Executive met at NCB headquarters, Hobart House.

Leading up to this meeting there had been a variety of significant events. The NUM Executive had taken a decision some weeks previously to withdraw from the joint consultative procedures with the NCB at all levels, because it was claimed that the latter were unwilling to provide the information the union was demanding.

Arthur Scargill had written to the NCB on 24 November 1982 about this. The documentation provided for the 24 January meeting fully explained, as far as I was concerned, the NCB's attitude to the supply of information to trade unions.

They accepted that it was their responsibility to provide such information about the industry's affairs so as to enable the trade unions to discharge their responsibilities to the members, or to be helpful to their members' understanding of the industry, and contribute to a joint resolution of any difficulties.

On the other hand, however, the NCB expected the unions to take a responsible attitude towards the use they made of information which, if published, could be detrimental to the industry, and consequently to union members.

Arthur Scargill had asked for copies of documents supplied to the Government body, the Monopolies and Mergers Commission, who were examining the industry, claiming that they contained names of collieries scheduled for closure. The NCB's brief stated categorically that no such names were contained in the documents. It went on to state that, subject to qualification on publication, if the NUM specified the information they would like to have on the topics covered by the brief, the NCB would do their best to supply it.

A further document was included in the brief, which gave an update of the current situation in the industry. This again specified that the Board did not have a programme of potential closures, and that the rate at which collieries came to the end of their useful lives must be determined locally by discussions between all parties.

After the meeting I reported my feelings to the Power Group, saying: 'I do feel, personally, that a more realistic atmosphere prevailed at the meeting with a recognition from all concerned that joint discussion within the industry was totally necessary if the problems are to be resolved in the interests of all.'

Unfortunately I also had to report that no decision had been taken on lifting the ban on consultation. There was mounting pressure against the ban from the membership, who did not take kindly to the elimination of their opportunity to discuss problems at pit level with management, with whom most had good relationships.

The days that followed were unhappy for me, and I was filled with a feeling of desolation when the following month, February 1983, Tom Bartle, General Secretary of the Durham Craftsmen's Association and the acknowledged leader of the right wing of the Executive, was fatally injured in a road accident. It was a great loss to the union and to me personally.

By 3 March 1983, the pit closure row was in the forefront of NEC debate again. At a special meeting on that day, with the South Wales coalfield on strike over the closure of Ty Mawr-Lewis Merthyr colliery, it was decided to ballot the members as to whether they were 'in favour of the National Executive Committee's recommendation that they be given authority to take industrial action to prevent the closure or partial closure of any pit, plant or unit, other than on the grounds of exhaustion, including those currently threatened in South Wales'.

The result of this ballot was declared at a meeting of the NEC on 10 March 1983 and, again, the membership had not supported strike action. Of the 195,494 valid votes, 118,954 (61 per cent) had voted aginst strike with 76,540 (39 per cent) for it. The NEC decided there was no point in continuing with the ban on consultation, but reminded the membership that the union's policy of opposition to pit or plant closures would remain in operation unless or until it was superseded by a decision of Conference.

It was clear that the NUM were on a collision course with the Thatcher Government via the NCB. It was also becoming increasingly obvious that such a confrontation would prove to be very costly for the miners.

In June 1983 the Tories were returned to power by an increased majority. Coal stocks were at a record level and there seemed to be little sympathy from the vast majority of the general public or from some leading trades unions for a union, like the NUM, which was headed by politically motivated militants. But the strike was still nine months away.

On 15 June a meeting was held between the NUM and the NCB to consider documentation presented the previous day to the Joint Policy Advisory Committee which consisted of both NCB and union members.

Reports were provided on the current situation and prospects for the year 1983-4, and there was a statement by Norman Siddall on a discussion document which had been a 'confidential report' to Government departments but which had already been the subject of much media speculation.

Again, the first brief was dealt with in the usual way, and the information was illustrated by slides.

Much debate took place on the separate items, I being particularly concerned with a claim that there were too many craftsmen in the industry which had resulted in an imbalance in relation to other categories of workers. I maintained that this was an invalid comparison and, bearing in mind increasing mechanization and technology, the numbers of craftsmen should be ascertained by reference to safety, required maintenance, manning levels and future requirements.

But inevitably, the pit closure issue started to dominate the meeting. Arthur Scargill again asked for three items. Firstly, the document which had been the subject of media reports; secondly, details of the NCB proposals for the rundown of the industry, area by area, pit by pit; and thirdly, all of the documents supplied to the MMC which had been asked for previously. It should be mentioned here that the NUM Executive had decided that neither they, nor membership at local levels, would participate in the MMC investigation.

Norman Siddall, replying to the President's three requests, said firstly the document was not a plan but a discussion document with Government departments; secondly, there were no details since they would be dealt with by area directors through the review procedures; and thirdly, he could not supply copies of documents for the same reasons as at the previous meeting, when it had been made clear that, only if the union made specific requests for details, would the NCB do its best to provide such information.

The NCB circulated a brief on the current situation and prospects for the year 1983-4, in particular referring to stocks in the country being at over 50 million tonnes and saying that one of the main factors for the worsening financial situation was the continued operation of collieries which, whilst accounting for only about 12 per cent of the industry's annual output, were persistently heavy losers – to the tune of some £250 million a year.

Budget proposals for the year had been set for area directors; the total saleable output was £318,000,000. The manpower budget, showing the workforce necessary to achieve the expected performance, was an average 196,300 which implied a manpower rundown during the year of about 12,000, or a loss over five years of 65,000 jobs.

'Some colliery closures will be inevitable,' the brief stated, 'but no specific assumptions have been made at national level on the extent to which closures may be necessary to achieve the budgets.' It also made clear that this document was 'intended to form a basis for further discussions with the Department of Energy at official level. It does not have the status of a corporate plan, since the strategy has not been agreed by Government, or detailed decisions taken by the Board.'

Arthur Scargill claimed in the media, following the meeting, that Norman Siddall's confirmation of the implications confirmed his own statements over the past year, that the NCB intended to cut 70,000 jobs and close seventy pits.

Norman Siddall, similarly reported in the media, categorically denied confirming that this meant the closure of seventy pits. The NCB had no 'hit-list' and no plans for closures. Closures were decided by area directors who discussed them with the unions.

On Thursday, 23 June 1983 – two weeks before the Annual Conference – the MMC report was published, which agreed with the NCB's view that the surplus production from high-cost, low-productivity pits was a crucial problem, and preventing the coal industry becoming viable. The Commission said, however, that it would not be appropriate for them to define precisely how to deal with the problem. Coincidentally, the NUM Executive met on the same day and decided on a campaign against closures.

At a press conference after the meeting, Arthur Scargill was reported in the *Guardian* as saying that the Executive would propose an emergency resolution to the union's Annual Conference in Perth the following month, recommending a massive coalfield campaign . . . leading eventually, if necessary, to a fourth ballot vote. He went on to say: 'We need the backing of our members because the next pit to be faced with closure could be theirs, the next job to be lost could be theirs. The union is not prepared to sit idly by and see this industry butchered.'

There was an electric atmosphere at the Conference which was held the first weekend in July and proved to have far-reaching consequences.

The Power Group had placed on the agenda a resolution which sought to change Rule 43. This rule reads:

43. – In the event of national action being proposed by the Union in pursuance of any of the objects of the Union, the following provision shall apply:–

That a national strike shall only be entered upon as the result of a ballot vote of the members taken in pursuance of a resolution of Conference, and a strike shall not be declared unless 55 per cent of those voting in the ballot vote in favour of such a strike. If a ballot vote be taken during the time a strike is in progress, a vote of 55 per cent of those taking part in the ballot shall be necessary to continue the strike.

If a ballot vote be taken during the time a stoppage is in progress, such stoppage may not be continued unless 55 per cent of those voting in the ballot vote in favour of continuance.

We wanted it to read that all industrial action, including an overtime ban, required an individual ballot vote of the membership. Three other areas of the union had placed similar resolutions on the agenda, but withdrew them in favour of the Power Group. Unfortunately a majority at Conference were against the resolution and so it was rejected.

However, a resolution from the Durham Craftsmen's Association and the Northumberland craftsmen opposing the placing of two items, such as pit closures and wages, on one ballot paper for one vote was successful. The resolution read that in future, 'national ballot papers should be worded in such a way that each question requires an individual answer, and at no time shall more than one question be put with provision for only one answer to be given.' This was well-supported and carried.

Two other resolutions formulated by the Executive at Conference were placed on the agenda as emergency resolutions and were carried. The first instructed the Executive and the NUM officials to embark immediately upon a campaign to win the wholehearted support of miners not only to oppose pit and works closures, but all reductions in manpower. The NUM Executive was further instructed to conduct a national ballot of members on the question of pit and works closures at a time deemed to be most appropriate. The second said that the NUM was totally opposed to the proposals for further trade union legislation contained in the Government green paper 'Democracy in Trade Unions', also known as the Tebbit Law. This is the name given to proposals, which are being gradually introduced, stating that ballots should be held within trade unions on the election of officials and the distribution of political funds.

'This is the most serious post-war attack upon the activities and legal integrity of trade unions, which utterly disregards the principles of both human and trade union rights enshrined in the International Labour Organisation conventions,' read the resolution.

Developments over the coming months were to lead members to believe that ballot papers were to be ignored completely and considered unnecessary, for the instructions of two Conference resolutions to hold ballots on pit closures and pay had been ignored and, far from it being the proposed Tebbit Law which disregarded the principles of trade union rights, many NUM members would be looking to some Government and the law to ensure their rights were respected.

On 1 September 1983, a naturalized American, Ian Mac-Gregor, became the new Chairman of the NCB. This was bound to be a provocative appointment when you consider that his previous appointment as head of the British Steel Corporation resulted in thousands of jobs being cut in order to make steel profitable again.

Arthur Scargill, commenting on the appointment, said:

> The union's concern was with the policy, not with the personalities. We have constantly warned that this man's mission is savagely to butcher the industry the way he has butchered British steel. I am not particularly concerned with who the Government selects as Chairman of the National Coal Board. The National Coal Board and the Tory government are already operating a pit closure programme by stealth. This will now be speeded up and the Siddall scalpel will be replaced by the MacGregor hatchet. I am convinced that miners will fight against the decimation of our industry.

I had taken a different view: I *was* concerned who the Government appointed, and particularly concerned that whoever it was should be acceptable to the miners. I had even written to the Prime Minister, Margaret Thatcher, purely on a personal basis and prior to the appointment, suggesting that in my opinion, Roy Mason, MP, a Labour minister in the Wilson and Callaghan Governments and also a former miner, would be ideally suited for the position and would create more cohesion among the moderate elements in the union. My plea had been acknowledged with an assurance that note would be taken of the suggestion.

I had nothing against Ian MacGregor personally, but I do think he was not a wise choice given the political climate within the NUM. I have met MacGregor several times, and always found him quite friendly and willing to answer questions. I remember, in particular, the time when he came to Bagworth in Leicestershire in November 1983. I was photographed with him when he came to declare open Asfordby, a new mine in the Vale of Belvoir near Bagworth.

The NUM side of the Joint National Negotiating Committee met at Hobart House in London on the morning of Tuesday, 27 September, and considered a document presenting the union's wage claim. The NCB gave their reply at a further meeting on Friday, 30 September. Their 'final' offer was a 5.2 per cent increase on national grade rates.

The following weekend was the Power Group's annual weekend school in Hanley, Stoke-on-Trent, and delegates were addressed on Sunday, 9 October by the President, Arthur Scargill.

Arthur described the offer of 5.2 per cent as an insult, ranging between £2.80 to £3 per week in take-home pay. 'It would take an average increase of 23 per cent just to restore the miners' wage to the 1974 values,' he said and went on to say that the men should ask their wives what they thought of the pay offer in relation to the cost of living increase.

'If you want wage increases to which you are entitled, and if you want to stop the closures of pits and save jobs, sooner or later you have got to give us the authority to carry through Conference resolutions,' he told the delegates.

He claimed that the industry was, in fact, making a profit, not a loss, because the 25 million tonnes of coal stocks at collieries had been undervalued by £8 a tonne and, because of that, the total accounts were £200 million undervalued. 'So instead of the loss last year, the Board made nearly £100 million profit,' he claimed. He said the high cost of stocking coal was also a factor and if the NCB reduced the price of coal and got rid of stocks, they would make a record profit. They would make even more if the industry had the same subsidies as did the coal mining industry of other European countries. The British coal industry was the most sophisticated in the world, he said, and added: 'It is rubbish to suggest we are uneconomic.'

Merrick Spanton, a Board member of the NCB, in reply, said that Britain could have the largest, most efficient deep-mine coal industry in Europe by the end of the century, but that depended on the closure of heavy loss-making pits and involved

May 1967. My last conference of the Transport and General Workers' Union before
I took over the reins of the newly-formed Power Group in the summer of that year.
I am in the back row, far right

I am held spellbound as Joe Gormley makes a point at the Power Group's Annual
Conference in 1971 – the year he became President of the NUM. Sitting by me
is Michael Carey, a great friend and colleague, who died a few years later

Joe Gormley took the NUM Executive to 10 Downing Street (above) at the end of 1973 for crucial talks with Prime Minister, Ted Heath, and to Hobart House (below), NCB headquarters, as the situation reached crisis proportions. But all the talking was in vain: the miners went on strike and the Heath Government fell in February 1974. Round the table at Hobart House (from left to right) is: NUM General Secretary Lawrence Daly, Vice-President Mick McGahey, President Joe Gormley, NCB Deputy Chairman Norman Siddall, and Head of Industrial Relations Cliff Shephard

continuous modernization of the rest of the industry.

Before the end of the week we received a circular from NUM head office setting out the result of negotiations and the convening of a Special Delegate Conference. Areas were requested to consider the possibility of imposing an overtime ban in the industry.

The day before this Conference, a joint meeting was arranged in London of the NUM Executive, the National Association of Colliery Overmen, Deputies and Shotfirers (NACODS), and the British Association of Colliery Management (BACM). The meeting had originally been suggested by NACODS, and the presidents of all three organizations emphasized the need for a common approach to the programme of the NCB to run down the coal industry, based on areas of mutual interest and policy.

It appeared at the time, and later became quite clear, that whilst the other two organizations agreed with the aims of the NUM, they did not agree with the tactics and strategy of industrial action, but rather wanted consultation and negotiation.

The next morning at the NUM Special Delegate Conference, held at the City University, London, it was unanimously agreed to reject the NCB's proposal on wages as totally unsatisfactory; to instruct the NUM Executive to continue negotiations to secure an improved offer; to reaffirm the union's opposition to all pit closures other than on the grounds of exhaustion, and to fight any further reduction in manpower levels; to resist the NCB/Government plans to close seventy pits over the coming five-year period; and to impose a full overtime ban from 31 October, 1983 as a first step in the campaign against the NCB's programme of attacks on jobs and living standards.

As a member of the Executive right up to this point, I have to accept the collective responsibility for decisions which were made. I cannot explain the failure of many of us to argue more vociferously against confrontation and in favour of consultation and negotiation. It is true that there was a school of thought, often voiced outside Executive meetings, which went along the lines of 'Let Arthur dig the hole big enough and he'll fall in.' I suppose too we had grown slightly complacent because we knew about the individual ballot vote contained in Rule 43, as I have mentioned before. Also there had been the three recent ballot votes which had rejected strike action over pay or pit closures. I also felt I had to some extent eased my conscience by warning my own Power Group Executive that if industrial action was entered into, as a result of the Conference, then membership would be facing the same situation as in 1926. It didn't take much to arrive at that conclusion, bearing in mind the fact that we had 53 million tonnes of stocks at power stations and pit heads, a determined Government, and little or no sympathy from the ranks of the trade unionists as deduced from the votes cast in the General Election of 1983, when many had voted Conservative. In any case, we were now bound by the decision of Conference and the organizational pattern of the NUM imposed restrictions on every individual's actions within the Executive.

The overtime ban started, liaison committees were formed within areas and many difficulties were encountered, with members at pits being laid off and losing pay because maintenance and repair work was done in the week and not at weekends as normal.

By the end of December 1983 I had a rebellion on my hands – from the Power Group's winding enginemen in North Staffordshire who operate the shaft cages. They were smarting from the fact that the overtime ban had been introduced without a ballot. The men were making national news when they threatened to start working weekends. This, they claimed, was their sixth shift, according to their six-day agreement, and not actual overtime.

I wrote to Arthur Scargill on 30 December 1983 explaining the situation and pointing out that the winders, who had been warned that they would be picketed at the pit gates, were retaliating by saying if picketing occurred, they would withdraw their labour for the following twenty-four hours which would prevent the total underground workforce in North Staffordshire from working during that period. I also advised Arthur that eleven Power Group branches had demanded a ballot on the wages issue, representing nearly half of the membership, and three branches had requested a ballot on both the wages issue and the overtime ban. 'I am concerned,' I wrote, 'that all of these situations are signifying growing rifts within the membership. I am firmly of the opinion that it would be sad for the members, and tragic for the union, if a sort of civil war broke out in the North Staffordshire coalfield. The winders are really only asking that they be given the opportunity to express their opinion in the democratic manner so jealously guarded previously in the NUM.'

Arthur replied at length. He drew attention to the decisions of the Special Delegate Conference that a full overtime ban be imposed and asked that the contents of the letter be conveyed to the members.

My forecast of civil war was about to materialize, and I was afraid for the individual winders who would be facing the picket lines on their own at the pit gates the following day.

Telephone messages arrived almost constantly during the morning and by the time that the evening newspaper arrived it was reporting, UGLY SCENES AS WINDERS BID TO DEFY BAN and PIT REBELS FACE ANGRY PICKETS.

Something had to be done, so a meeting of the Power Group Executive was convened for Monday, 9 January. But this did not prevent the winders from carrying out their threat to hold a twenty-four hour strike which effectively laid off 5,000 miners in North Staffordshire. At the meeting the Power Group Executive suspended the winding enginemen from the union and disbanded the branch, hoping to nullify their action. Although the winders did not attempt to work weekends afterwards, they nevertheless succeeded in obtaining legal opinion to justify their claim that the union's actions had been 'against the principles of natural justice'. The branch and all its members were reinstated, and they have constantly tried to obtain what they considered to be their right: a democratic ballot.

Their action was the first sign of rebellion from the NUM membership and foreshadowed what was to happen in 1984 in areas like Nottingham, Leicester, South Derbyshire and the Midlands with miners defying strike action and going to work.

Despite this rebellious behaviour the Power Group Executive were behind me on one issue: they had endorsed my personal plea to Arthur to hold a ballot.

Arthur didn't respond to my request. And I wasn't really that surprised when later I learned in the *Daily Mail* on 13 January in reply to a question about seeking a proper pithead vote that he had the nerve to say: 'We haven't had a single request for it.'

– 3 –
The Fateful Meeting

It was 8 March 1984, NUM Executive meeting day, which is always the second Thursday in the month.

I was driving to the NUM headquarters in Sheffield.* As I drove I tried to anticipate what might happen about the overtime ban, which had been in operation since the previous October, and was causing many problems, with men throughout nearly all the coalfields being sent home and losing pay due to lack of maintenance at the pits. Pressures were building up to such an extent that very deep consideration would have to be given towards negotiating an end to the action.

In my mind I went over recent events. There had been an indication of the attitude of the rank-and-file members some two weeks before when, according to reports in the Press, miners in Scotland at a Special Delegate Conference had rejected calls for strike action to save Polmaise Colliery. It had been reported that delegates from several large pits in the area had made it clear that they could not marshal support for what would amount to an escalation of the overtime ban. This was despite a campaign which had been spearheaded by the Scottish area leaders. Mick McGahey had been reported as stating, 'Pressure is building up for a strike in Scotland and we will be campaigning for action at the pithead. I can understand the men's anger and it has to be channelled to the Coal Board.'

More recently, on the other hand, a number of strikes had begun, all for different reasons. In Yorkshire, the Manvers,

* The NUM had moved out of 222 Euston Road and to Arthur's home county nearly a year earlier, in April 1983.

Wath and Kilnhurst Collieries were on strike in protest against proposed shift changes and starting times for men working on the surface at Manvers; and other pits in South Yorkshire were instructed to come and in support by the NUM South Yorkshire panel. Goldthorpe and Yorkshire Main Collieries were on strike over minor issues unrelated to the overtime ban. Bulcliffe Wood Colliery in the Barnsley area was on strike in protest against the allocation of some reserves from a nearby colliery, while in Scotland, Seafield Colliery was on strike over the disciplining of a craftsman and Polmaise was now on strike over the colliery's proposed closure.

On 1 March came the controversial decision by the South Yorkshire Area Director which escalated industrial action. He indicated that Cortonwood, an unprofitable colliery with a limited life expectancy of some five years, whose output of coking coal was no longer wanted by the British Steel Corporation, should cease production in April, subject to continuing discussions within the colliery review procedure which allowed the unions the opportunity to contest such a proposal, employing their own mining engineers and culminating in a final meeting in Room 16, Hobart House. This is of course the room in which we hold our meetings with the NCB. This sort of meeting, in fact is commonly known as 'a Room 16 appeal'. However, the proposal was not referred by the NUM for further discussion as would normally have been the case.

There had also been a meeting on 6 March of the Coal Industry National Consultative Council, at which all unions – BACM, NACODS and the NUM – were represented, and a joint paper, containing the proposals of the individual unions and the NCB, had been presented.

The immediate reaction of the unions to the need to bring about a further reduction in output to bring supply and demand into balance was one of extreme concern, but there was no discussion on how this might be changed or any alternative way in which the industry's problems might be resolved. The NUM had said again that they would oppose any closures other than on the grounds of exhaustion.

The proposals of the NCB and the unions were also intended

to bring about a measure of agreement between all parties towards a tripartite meeting with Government.

Budgets for the year 1984-5 had been presented, showing a reduction of 4 million tonnes of deep-mined revenue output compared with the previous year. The greatest reductions were to be in the Scottish, North-East and South Wales coalfields. The budget also predicted that only North Nottingham, Barnsley, North Yorkshire, South Yorkshire and North Derbyshire would make a profit – £96.2 million total – the remaining seven NCB areas being expected to suffer a loss of £200.7 million.

Subsequently, the NUM Executive met the NCB, chaired now by Ian MacGregor, so that all those who were not present as representatives could be fully informed as to what had transpired. A summary was given, and Arthur Scargill argued that by using the budget figures for the preceding year of 105.6 million tonnes, the NCB were effectively budgeting for a reduction of 8 million tonnes in 1984-5. This was the information on which he again based his argument to project seventy pit losses and 70,000 jobs.

Then, over the first weekend in March, NUM branch meetings at eight of the fifteen South Yorkshire pits voted not to join the strike called for the following Monday. Nevertheless, on 5 March, all but four pits in South Yorkshire were prevented from working as men refused to cross picket lines and the following day all fifteen pits were either picketed out or on strike.

The same day, a special council meeting of the Yorkshire NUM decided to call a strike across the whole of Yorkshire from 9 March, in protest against what they called 'the Coal Board's decision to escalate the attack upon our industry'.

Meanwhile, I had contacted all branches in the Power Group letting them have all the latest documentation I had on the spreading dispute and telling them: 'It is difficult to anticipate developments at the NEC in the light of reported actions in Yorkshire and Scotland, but I assure you of my intention not to agree with any strike action until a ballot of the membership has taken place in accordance with the rules.'

I had long realized I was in the middle of history-making

decisions. Democracy within the NUM seemed to be slowly slipping away, and I felt helpless to stem the course of events which was destroying everything I had worked for throughout my career.

Arriving at NUM headquarters – located in the top three floors of a large office block, built of concrete and glass – we all took our places in the big conference room. This room, unlike the former NUM Executive meeting room in London, with its leather armchairs and engraved windows, is an impersonal room, lacking in atmosphere. We seemed to sit a long way from each other and have to shout rather than talk. Through the large picture windows you could see the rooftops of neighbouring buildings. The view on a clear day was quite spectacular.

The meeting was opened by the President, Arthur Scargill. He welcomed Peter Heathfield as the newly-elected General Secretary, and Gilbert Butler who was replacing Peter Heathfield as the North Derbyshire representative.

The fateful meeting started in an ordinary way, like hundreds of other meetings. One of the early items on the agenda was the pay and conditions of canteen women. Details were then given of meetings that had taken place between the triple alliance unions – rail, steel and coal – regarding coal imports, and there were general questions arising out of the continuation of the overtime ban.

Information was also given on meetings of the emergency sub-committee that had taken place, concerning the coal stock situation at the pitheads. There were around 23,373,000 tonnes there, with the same amount also stocked at power stations.

Then, however, the ordinariness of the meeting abruptly changed. My attention was suddenly concentrated more acutely when it was stated that letters had been received from Scottish and Yorkshire areas calling for recognition by the NUM Executive of strikes in those areas. Scotland's action was over the proposed closure of Polmaise Colliery and Yorkshire's related to the NCB's proposal to close Cortonwood. Both wanted their actions sanctioned under Rule 41, which reads as follows:

41. – In the event of a dispute arising in any Area or applying to the workers in any Branch likely or possible to lead to a stoppage of work or any other industrial action short of a strike the questions involved must be immediately reported by the appropriate official of the Area in question to the National Executive Committee which shall deal with the matter forthwith, and in no case shall a cessation of work or other form of industrial action short of a strike take place by the workers without the previous sanction of the National Executive Committee, or of a Committee (whether consisting of members of the National Executive Committee or of other persons) to whom the National Executive Committee may have delegated the power of giving such sanction, either generally or in a particular case and no funds of the Union shall be applied in strike pay or other trades dispute benefit for the benefit of workers who shall have ceased work without the previous sanction of the National Executive Committee.

Yorkshire had called the strike from the following day, urging support from all areas within the union.

The North Western NUM area, Lancashire, had also submitted a letter from their Executive about the Cronton Colliery closure and calling for the go-ahead for an immediate ballot vote of the members in the area to support strike action.

Straightaway I smelled a rat. I realized the Yorkshire and Scottish calls could represent the start of a national strike without a ballot. It was obvious that Britain's miners were in danger of being brought out through mass-picketing and intimidation. The sickening part was that it was all so predictable. The alarm bells had already sounded when I had heard Mick McGahey saying on the news on television that 'We will not be constitutionalized out of action.' Though I have often admired Mick as a statesman, this is the sort of behaviour I find difficult to accept.

Arthur Scargill then put the contents of the letters open for debate and Eric Clarke, Secretary of the Scottish area, immediately jumped in, stating in his usual dogmatic manner that their delegate meeting had given the officials the right to escalate the present action of the overtime ban and that therefore they would be on strike from the following Monday. It was his contention that Polmaise was a developing colliery although the NCB was contending that geology, ash content and other factors were the problems associated with the pit. He said the Scottish Colliery Enginemen and Boiler Trades Association (the Scottish NUM craftsmen) were united with them and that all areas should unite.

'There is no alternative but to fight for our existence, and we hope that the other unions and other communities will join us.'

He concluded by attacking the new redundancy payments announcements made by the NCB that morning and released to the media. Under these terms £1,000 per year of service would be given to any miner who chose to leave the industry as an alternative to being transferred to another colliery.

From the mood of the meeting I sensed that the miners' basic democratic rights were under increasing pressure, especially when Sid Vincent put forward his views. He said there was a simple reason for the letter from Lancashire: there was a serious danger of the men bringing down the present action on overtime by breaking the ban. They had only just managed at their delegate conference to get a decision to approach the NUM Executive for a strike ballot over Cronton. He added, however, that he believed a ballot in the area would not have supported strike action. 'Personally I believe it is now or never. I don't know how we are going to do it, because behind the figures presented there is a monster.'

One could only presume that the 'monster' he was referring to was the men not wanting to strike.

Jack Taylor, the Yorkshire area President, made it clear that the decision to strike in Yorkshire had not been taken lightly. It was possible that there would be opposition to the decision which could lead to a reaction and bring the overtime ban to an end in the county.

'We are not naive,' he said and, referring to the dispute in Yorkshire, said the situation had resulted from a problem about Manvers' meal times and that the manager had sent letters to all the men giving an ultimatum that they would be sent home. He said there followed a colliery review meeting at area level. Cortonwood was the last item on the agenda, and this was an economic closure. Jack also claimed that the NCB Area

Director in Yorkshire had been ordered to reduce coal production. 'It is a farcical situation,' he said, and stressed there had been an 86 per cent area vote for action in a ballot in 1981. Cortonwood was not militant, he went on, but they had decided unanimously to fight, and industrial action had been called. The action was supported by all branches in the area who had so far had meetings.

'It is not just an issue for us,' he continued, 'we could have kept our heads down. After all, we have got the new developments at Selby and Thorne [two sophisticated new coalfields in Yorkshire].' He said Cortonwood would come out on Monday but he could not guarantee if all in the area would.

'Even if we don't get your support we shall win Cortonwood on our own. The redundancy money offered is because the Board and the Government are worried that you will support us. We don't believe either BACM or NACODS will support us but we are going to put them in a position where they will have to fight. We are on our way.'

I found it quite astonishing that an area would use a three-year-old ballot to back up action. But it turned out to be a meeting which brought one shocking statement after another.

Abe Moffat, son of the former leader of the Scottish miners, spoke next. He represented the Scottish Craftsmen's area, and briefly repeated the call made by Eric Clarke.

Then Henry Richardson, General Secretary of the Nottinghamshire miners, put his point of view. He had been verbally attacked by the lobbyists outside when entering the building. He said the men in Nottingham had been loyal to the overtime ban and if the action was going to be escalated, it would be supported.

'But,' he continued defiantly, 'calling us scabs will not help us. I have been called that already outside. If Notts are scabs before we start, Notts will become scabs. You will make our jobs [as area officials] impossible.'

Jack Jones, Leicestershire miners' General Secretary, said in reply that while he sympathized with his dilemma, the position was not new. The success of the overtime ban had hit the NCB and the Government's economic position. 'I don't know what the National Officials' position is, but if we continue the overtime ban until October, then we could fight on our own ground.' He said the country had a determined Government. A strike had got to have the support of all trade unions, for only the downfall of the Government would see miners win or bring about a change in economic policy.

'We have got to be sure we have the support of all. We have to know that we have them to be certain we are not in the same position as in 1926.'

Jack said he was perturbed as to how the NUM Executive would go about it. 'We were consulted on the overtime ban and although Yorkshire have the right to ask under Rule 41, I prefer we do it under Rule 43. We have to have the sanction of our members.'

The President of the Northumberland miners, Denis Murphy, also spoke in favour of a ballot within Rule 43.

'I agree with Jack Jones and I also support Henry Richardson. And another thing – we don't want pickets from Yorkshire or anywhere. You keep your men within Yorkshire and Scotland,' he said.

Trevor Bell was the next to speak, and referred to the statement from the NCB on both wages and closures. He said both were 'positive' (i.e. final) and no retraction likely. There was not only Cronton and Cortonwood to consider, he went on, but Durham and Northumberland were affected and really ought to be able to get support.

'I suggest we have enough before us to persuade our members. I propose that we go out to ballot our members on pay and closures. And let me say this, it did not help when Mick McGahey made his statement on television that we would not be constitutionalized out of action.'

Trevor's resolution read:

> In the light of the announcement by the NCB last Tuesday to implement a further savage new rundown in mining including the closure of over twenty pits and the loss of 20,000 jobs, the NUM Executive agrees to consult the members in a national ballot on wages and pit closures under Rule 43, with a recommendation for strike action.

Emlyn Williams immediately came into the debate, apparently motivated by Trevor Bell's motion. He did not argue for a ballot. Instead he moved that the NUM Executive endorse the requests made by the areas in the letters. 'The fight in South Wales will be for the survival of South Wales. It is going to be difficult, but the scenario has changed since MacGregor's statement,' he said.

He then moved his formal resolution to back the Scottish and Yorkshire strikes, a resolution which I felt had been prepared for the meeting. It appeared, also, that he was not too sure of his members' reactions in his own area.

Ken Toon then intervened with the question: 'How are we going to alter the overtime ban action to other action? No pit is safe but we went the right way on the overtime ban.'

He went on to analyse the effect of the overtime ban in his own area, and expressed concern about using Rule 41 for further action.

'Areas have got to have time,' he said. 'Some in my area will jump to support, but there are others who won't. We need a ballot but I recognize there is no hope if [action in] Yorkshire dies.'

Ray Chadburn said he agreed with what had been said by all, but also said that people outside had accused him of destroying the union when he had been totally committed to the overtime ban.

'There are three areas with requests but I reflect the views of my own people. Like them I object to Mick McGahey throwing out the constitution. Our members are throwing the constitution at us now and they want a ballot.

'We may be able to get around it but before a strike takes place we have to have a ballot. Our mandate must be to work at it with conferences in the areas, and with a secret ballot in Notts I think we could win. We have to be extremely careful, and already we have told our members not to cross picket lines.'

Ted McKay said: 'There is a difference between Yorkshire and Lancashire in their letters of request and I want to make the point that picketing is intimidation. I am also concerned about McGahey's statement about not being constitutionalized out of action. We want a ballot.'

Charles Barlow, an agent (a fulltime official representing a part of an area) for the Midlands area miners, said: 'I find myself at a disadvantage. We have had no council meetings.' He said the overtime ban had been successful and that if others had operated it with the rigidity the Midlands area had, the effect would have been better.

'But there is a constitutional position and we have to ballot the members. I also criticize Mick McGahey for his statement and Rule 43 has got to be the position. I take exception to Yorkshire and Scotland booing me outside. I shall seek to get support for them but we must have a ballot.'

Wesley Chambers, lay member representative for the Kent area, spoke next, his words reflecting the tough, undemocratic way in which that area always seems to operate: 'It is a national situation, but if we have got to have ballots we are starting to lose. We have got to get a chance in energy policy and the Kent area will be out from Monday.'

Ron Dunn, Durham Craftsmen's representative, was clear and to the point: 'We have a rule book and the members are the custodians. It is a dangerous path to support Yorkshire and Scotland and we shall get pockets of resistance. Let's have the correct procedure of a ballot.'

Bill Stobbs, Durham area miners' lay member representative, was even more forthright. He said simply: 'Our men will be out on Monday.'

It was time for me to say my piece on behalf of Power Group members and, indeed, all the members of the union who, it seemed to me, were being betrayed by those who were not prepared to consult them through an individual ballot.

I spoke for a ballot on both the pit closure and wages questions and seconded Trevor Bell's proposal that a national individual ballot vote be taken. I referred to the difficulties experienced with the winding engineers in North Staffordshire and explained I had written to Arthur Scargill, saying it would be sad for the members and tragic for the union if a sort of civil war broke out in the Staffordshire coalfield.

I told the meeting: 'I have little doubt that if you take a decision today under Rule 41, then the strike will lead to civil war throughout the union and the country. In any case I am not prepared to disfranchise the members in Scotland and Yorkshire or any other area in the union.'

Harry Hanlon, Cumberland area General Secretary, said: 'There has got to be some change in tactics but we shall not hold any other ballot than a national one!'

Gilbert Butler, North Derbyshire representative, did not commit himself, saying: 'We are in a different situation. We have not had meetings but we can convey to meetings what has been expressed here. I have a question. Do we picket deputies?'

His question seemed to indicate that only those expressions at the meeting for strike action would be conveyed.

Idwal Morgan, the cokemen's General Secretary who had just replaced the former General Secretary, Harry Close, two months earlier, made what I thought seemed hardly consistent with the members' constitutional rights. He said. 'If I had the confidence that a [national] ballot would go the right way, I would vote for it. But it will be in the hands of high incentive earners and those who want to be redundant. We should support Lancashire, Yorkshire and Scotland, and I know that I will have to try to get that support. But, we should ignore the individual ballot.'

Owen Briscoe, the Yorkshire General Secretary, said: 'I hope there is no defeatism talk when we go out of here.' He said there were 20,000 jobs to go a year in the industry and now the NCB were offering £1,000 a year to those who opted for redundancy.

He added: '£20,000 to £30,000 for redundants takes some refusing, but I ask the NEC to look carefully at the Yorkshire tradition and I ask for support for both Yorkshire and Scotland.'

He was, in fact, perfectly right about it being hard for redundants to choose. He and others were hardly giving them a chance to choose.

I was reflecting on the changes I had seen in the Yorkshire area during my years on the NUM Executive – the main one being that this traditionally moderate area was now being led by militants – when the last speaker, George Rees, came into the discussion. And when George speaks in his usual loud and forceful manner, everybody hears. He said it would be difficult to change those areas with 80 per cent against strike in the last ballot to a 55 per cent majority.

'You are not being honest when you say we should adhere to the rule book. They are not all in favour in South Wales but we are all elected to represent our members. Are you afraid to persuade your members by standing up and telling them? You should get your members out and then come back for endorsement. You will have the Press and media against you in a ballot. I am being parochial. Get back and fight for what you believe in,' he concluded.

I remember wanting to do some shouting of my own – in protest over what George Rees had said. And maybe I should have. But I kept quiet, and thought of the only bit of Latin I know, *Quot homines, tot sententiae,* which I believe means, 'There are as many opinions as there are men.'

Twenty-two members of the NUM Executive had spoken. Those who had not were the three NUM officials – Arthur Scargill, Peter Heathfield and Mick McGahey – and one lay member from Yorkshire, John Weaver.

It was now time for the President, Arthur Scargill, to wind up the debate. Being custodian of the rules, he should, in my opinion, have ruled that a ballot vote of the members be taken if the intention was to escalate the action from an overtime ban into a national strike.

Alternatively, if Yorkshire and Scotland areas' action was to be sanctioned, then there should be no picketing. It was up to all areas to decide themselves what action they wished to take. After all, as President, he had Conference decisions to guide him. And he had stated on more than one occasion that he would 'not allow Conference decisions to be trivialized'.

The two relevant Conference decisions, carried at the 1983 Annual Conference in Perth, both referred to a ballot of the membership. The Special Delegate Conference held in London on 18 October 1983, which had imposed the overtime ban, had considered the resolutions. Surely, I now asked myself, it was now the appropriate time for the members to be consulted in a ballot?

It was not to be. Arthur demonstrated which side he was on.

It was clear he wanted strike action and he was determined not to be thwarted yet again by the members deciding for themselves.

He wound up the debate by saying the 'constitution' was simple. There was Trevor Bell's proposal which had been seconded for a strike ballot, and there was Emlyn Williams' proposal for the Executive to support the action in Yorkshire and Scotland.

'I only want to make one or two points, but there is one simple fact of life,' said Arthur. He went on to say that there were 179 pits plus workshops and coking plants and, according to the NCB's figures, 115 of them were uneconomic.

'This debate will be meaningless unless the union takes some decisions. It is now the crunch time. We are all agreed we have to fight. We have an overtime ban. It is only the tactics which are at question.'

He then put the proposal of Emlyn Williams to the vote. There were twenty-one votes for, with only three votes against: Trevor Bell's, Ted McKay's and my own.

I was surprised that only three of us had voted for democracy, considering how many of the others had spoken up for a ballot in the debate. But that was it. The NUM Executive, by a majority in accordance with Rule 41, had declared the proposed strike action in Yorkshire and Scotland and in any other area which took similar action as official.

Arthur subsequently informed the media that the decision was unanimous by virtue of a substantive motion. It even appeared so later in the minutes of the meeting. Another devious move, I thought to myself.

– 4 –
Sparks Fly

Feeling totally dejected, I realized I was approaching the stage when I would be forced to take matters into my own hands. Self-respect dictated that I must not accept a situation which I found to be alien to everything I had stood for in the union. But such troubled thoughts were pushed to the back of my mind for the time being. The NUM Executive meeting, the memories of which will remain with me for the rest of my life, had come to a close. The meeting had lasted five hours, considerably longer than usual. But I had little time to ponder on the events; there were more shocks to come.

At about 3 pm, we were required to drive across Sheffield to a hotel where all the finance officers within the NUM had been called to a meeting. We were told it would clear up 'blind decisions' we had taken – at Arthur's request – during the Executive meeting in the morning when we formally accepted the minutes of decisions of the NUM Finance and General Purposes Committee, of which I and some of my colleagues were not members. Arthur had presented these minutes and asked us to accept them without giving us any information.

The meeting certainly cleared a lot of matters up for me, not the least being that I had absolute confirmation that not only had there been collusion between Yorkshire and Scotland to get strike action, but steps had been taken by the NUM officials and union trustees to prevent possible sequestration of union funds well before any decision to strike.

Whilst not given to blind loyalty, I was secure in the knowledge that there were some colleagues at least who had been present at the Finance and General Purposes Committee meeting held the previous day, who would know what the relevant minutes meant.

But some of the decisions minuted were puzzling to say the least.

1. Mr S. Thompson and Mr H. Richardson had resigned as Trustees of the union and it was agreed that in accordance with Rule 21 Mr McGahey and Mr Scargill be appointed Trustees to fill the casual vacancies.

2. It was agreed that the National Union Secretary and Trustees be given authority to invest the funds of the union in any joint Stock Bank and its subsidiaries.

3. It was agreed that the report of the National Officials be accepted and that assets to the value of £1,000,000 be settled upon the Trust for education and other benefits and that areas be permitted similarly to establish trusts if deemed desirable.

Much of the talking at this meeting of finance officers and NEC members was done by the union's Chief Executive Officer, Roger Windsor, later to become well known for his fund-raising visit to Colonel Ghaddafi in Libya.

The meeting was held in a large room with a long table at one end and tall windows at the other, draped with closed curtains reaching to the floor. While we were having tea and sandwiches from the long table waiting for the NUM officials to arrive, Roger Windsor, much to my amusement, kept peering behind the curtains. I don't know what he expected to find – some spies maybe – but his behaviour certainly helped to set the scene for what was to be a mysterious meeting conducted in undertones.

An area finance officer, who telephoned me two or three days later for information on what action we had taken in the Power Group, started to laugh, almost hysterically, swearing blind that Roger Windsor had picked up an empty matchbox, looked inside as though expecting to find an electronic bug, and then thrown it down again.

Arthur had opened the meeting, Peter Heathfield and Mick McGahey sitting either side of him.

In a quiet voice, obviously intended to convey the seriousness and secrecy with which the discussions had to be treated, he told us about the implications of industrial relations legislation, under which all trade unions were liable at law to sequestration of funds if an injunction were secured through the courts. Such sequestration did not apply merely to national funds, but also to area and branch funds.

It was quite clear from this introduction that, although the NUM Executive had only sanctioned strikes in Yorkshire and Scotland at this stage, there was an intention knowingly to breach the law – by secondary picketing or otherwise – which would make the Yorkshire and Scottish area funds subject to sequestration. One had to presume also that the NUM officials would be complying with Yorkshire and Scottish actions, thereby bringing national funds into risk.

A further problem was outlined to the effect that any unlawful action committed by an individual member or group of members would need to be condemned and not simply voted against if legal decisions were to be avoided.

The property of the union would also be at stake and all full-time officials could, if thought to be acting contrary to the law, have their property, house, car, goods and money seized.

There really was no need to tell me this or, indeed, tell many of the others present. If you break the law, then you pay for it.

However, Roger Windsor then related the story of the seventy-year-old National Graphical Association trustee who, during the NGA's industrial action, had purged his contempt of the law to avoid sequestration of his property. He went on, still in undertones, to say that it really was a serious matter, and that while they were not advising breaking the laws of the land, that even this meeting could be considered conspiratorial.

I thought he was teetering on the edge of amateur dramatics at this point. I personally was not conspiring with anybody. I was just listening, and up to now, had taken no decision to break the law and didn't intend to do so anyway.

He stated that the funds of the union could be secured by the establishment of a charitable trust and, according to their current information, provided such trust deeds were made irrevocable, then the funds in trust would not be sequestrable. The NUM had, over the course of the last year, already decided to establish a trust for educational purposes, and that avenue could be pursued. Therefore, we were told, areas could settle all their assets, including property, in such a trust but it should be done within twenty-four hours.

This was another indication that picketing action was to be undertaken immediately and had been secretly decided upon prior to the NUM Executive decision on strike action.

It was then explained to all present that two of the trustees, Henry Richardson and Sam Thompson, had resigned and that Arthur Scargill and Mick McGahey had filled the casual vacancies and were therefore now in the 'firing line'.

There was one other way of safeguarding funds, said Windsor, but it was not being advocated. This was to liquidate all assets – gilts and bonds could take twenty-one days to be liquidated, they said – and place them beyond the jurisdiction of the courts. Jurisdiction of the courts only extends to the United Kingdom, it was said, and in any case the more you confuse the trail the better. There is only one safe place and that is cuckoo-clock land (he meant Switzerland presumably).

Investigations were being conducted to see whether the weekly deduction of union contributions, deducted by the NCB and remitted to the union, could be seized, but, said Roger Windsor: 'When the court made the order on the NGA, in two minutes flat, by a simple phone call, all their assets were frozen.' His tone of voice made me feel like a conspirator.

He added: 'All of you should now go and take what action your areas decide after consulting your solicitors and accountants.'

We were then given telephone numbers of three firms of solicitors who would be helpful, but we were told that if we needed advice from Roger Windsor personal contact only should be made with him even if that meant jumping in the car over the next twenty-four hours and going to see him. It seemed we really were in the realms of James Bond: a world of spies and phone-tapping. The intrigue deepened when it was stated that some banks in the Midlands were 'likely to be helpful'.

The whole meeting had been purely advisory, no decisions were made whatsoever, because the meeting had no power to do so. The fact that it took place at all has never been officially acknowledged.

It was quite clear though that the 'blind decision' taken by the Executive, at Arthur's request, had given Peter Heathfield and the trustees the authority to invest the funds of the union in joint stock banks and subsidiaries, with no need for them to come back to the Executive.

Months later, following high court decisions to fine the union, and Arthur Scargill individually for contempt of the law – a contempt which prompted my resignation from the Executive – we were to learn, from sequestrators appointed to levy the fines, of the various methods that had been used by the national officials and trustees in an attempt to place the union funds out of reach.

I drove home, intent upon consulting solicitors and accountants before morning, so as to be able to report to the Power Group Executive as quickly as possible.

The group's accountant and solicitor came to my home that night. Apart from deciding to contact the solicitors whose telephone numbers had been given, we reached the conclusion soon after midnight that there was little point in implementing the action which we had been advised to take.

The simple fact was that funds were not at risk if one didn't break the law. Secondly, if one 'salted away' the money then it would not be ready at hand to keep the organization going and, if any fines were imposed, sooner or later they would be levied when eventually the funds were brought back.

This latter fact has, I believe, now registered with most people in the union, although, since my retirement from the scene, a Special Delegate Conference has dealt with the subject. I believe at some stage the fines imposed on the union will be collected.

The next morning, 9 March, I reported to my Executive. First, I read them my notes of the proceedings of the NUM Executive meeting and they were absolutely astounded, and angry that a ballot vote had not been decided on. They were also amazed that, after what had been said in the morning, only three votes had been cast against the sanctioning of the strikes in Yorkshire and Scotland.

My action at the meeting was fully endorsed, and a statement was developed for circulation to Power Group members, in which the Executive demanded 'that the NUM Executive institute immediately the required procedures for a national individual ballot vote calling upon the members to take strike action'.

The statement went on to advise all members to abide by trade union principles and not cross picket lines, and a copy of it was sent immediately to Peter Heathfield.

My Executive also accepted the advice of the Group's accountant and solicitor and took no action to 'salt away' funds.

That night, feeling shattered, I travelled to Birmingham at the invitation of the BBC 'Newsnight' team and argued the case for a ballot, appearing on television with my colleague Terry Thomas, Vice-President of the South Wales area, who argued the case against.

I could tell my arguments fell on stony ground as far as Terry was concerned. I wasn't surprised because he had more than likely been involved in the developing of the resolution proposed by his area President, Emlyn Williams, at the NUM Executive meeting the previous day.

I also realized he would be reluctant to give any concession in the direction of a ballot vote, because this would be seized upon by many members in South Wales who were not in favour of supporting strike action. When both Emlyn and George Rees believed in the neccessity of strike action this was quite out of the question.

In the next few weeks picketing started. It soon reached such a pitch that it forced men out of pits while they were waiting for the result of their own area ballot vote. With flying pickets on the move and the Nottinghamshire coalfield virtually under siege, the NUM was in what I can only describe as a tragic state.

Over the weekend of 10 and 11 March, meetings were held at pits in Kent, South Wales, Scotland, the North East, Durham and Northumberland to decide whether to support the Yorkshire call.

Unsurprisingly, Kent joined the strike immediately, but a

majority of branches in South Wales and a number in Scotland and the North East decided that they would not.

The men's wish to have a democratic vote was just swept aside. Pits in Scotland were picketed and by 14 March they were all on strike. Collieries in the North East were on strike or picketed out by 15 March, as were all collieries in South Wales.

It was on 15 March that the Power Group President, Bob MacSporran, and Vice-President, Jim Dowling, led more than 250 Power Group craftsmen in a lobby to the NUM headquarters in Sheffield to demand a ballot. 'We want to see Arthur Scargill and put our views over to him,' said Jim. 'I am sure the majority of men in the union want a ballot. It is the democratic right of the members and the only way to bring unity to the pits again.'

The Power Group Executive had decided that under no circumstances would they personally conduct a ballot, for this was the responsibility of the NUM under Rule 43. By this time – the middle of March – it was estimated that 132 pits were on strike with 42 still working.

Obviously, it was impossible to determine how many of those miners not working stayed away because of picketing, but my worst suspicions – that we were embarking on civil war – were certainly being confirmed. A high level of policing was necessary to ensure that men who wished to work were able to do so.

On 12 March the Power Group Executive had met, and I had been instructed to write to Peter Heathfield. I wrote: 'They have instructed me to place before you a request that a special National Executive Committee meeting be convened to implement the request of the Power Group area that a national individual ballot vote be held calling upon the members to take strike action.'

Arthur knew that they were coming: indeed, he had telephoned me that morning in the office to ask me to stop them.

'Mr Scargill for you,' Janice, my secretary, had said. She switched him through.

'Two points,' said Arthur. 'First, your pension. I have the calculations and I'm sure you will be happy. Now the second point: can you stop this lobby coming to Sheffield this morning?'

In fact, I had already tried to do this: I feared they would be confronted by hundreds of Yorkshire pickets, and I worried for their safety. Arthur was worried that the media would report that everyone – Yorkshire pickets included – was demanding a ballot. By this time, though, it was too late: the men were on their way.

In the event, there were no Yorkshire pickets at headquarters. Most probably, Arthur had called them off after his conversation with me.

On arriving in Sheffield, Bob MacSporran and Jim Dowling headed a delegation which spent an hour with Arthur Scargill. They put over their views and, of course, they fell on deaf ears. But at least they did not exchange cross words.

The only cross words came later when Arthur went out on the steps to address the men and told them to get off their knees and fight. Understandably, the remark was met by heckling from the craftsmen. Arthur lost his temper and started to shout.

In my opinion, he shouldn't have shouted: these men were helping to pay his wages, and all they wanted was an equal say in how the union was run – surely not too much to ask.

One of the men remarked afterwards: 'We were happy in that we had made an effort. We were the only ones to lobby the headquarters and if some of the other areas had done the same, we may have had a ballot.'

On the same day, the Yorkshire area NUM Executive decided to ignore a High Court injunction sought by the NCB to stop picketing outside the Yorkshire area.

The night before, a young Yorkshire picket had collapsed and died in Nottinghamshire. In an effort to persuade Yorkshire area not to send pickets, Nottinghamshire NUM leaders had agreed that their own striking men in the area would picket their own pits. We also received a tele-message from their General Secretary, Henry Richardson, telling us that the area would be conducting a ballot of their own on Friday, 16 March and asking all areas not to send pickets to Nottinghamshire.

In fact, ballots were held in several NUM areas, none of which reached the 55 per cent majority which was the required percentage by NUM rules at that time for strike action. The results were:

NUM Area	% For strike	% Against strike
Cumberland	22	78
North Derbyshire	50	50
Leicestershire	11	89
Durham Winding Enginemen	15	85
South Derbyshire	16	84
Nottinghamshire	27	73
North Wales	32	68
Northumberland	52	48
North West (Lancs)	41	59
Midlands	27	73

Some other small areas also conducted ballots. The figures were not published but they were against strike action.

On 20 March we received a further tele-message from Henry Richardson, Nottinghamshire General Secretary, stating that, in view of the ballot vote recently taken in Nottinghamshire, a meeting of branch officials and committee members had decided to instruct the men to return to work as from the day shift on Monday, 19 March.

On 22 March, the Power Group Executive decided to write to both Arthur Scargill and Peter Heathfield with the same message as before, but informing them that all NUM Executive Committee members would be sent the following letter:

Dear Colleagues,
    You are fully aware that Power Group policy has been that of conforming to National Rule 43, thus ensuring that the membership determine by individual ballot vote their attitude to national strike action.
    So that you are fully aware of the actions taken by the Power Group area, I am instructed to let you have the attached copies of letters to Mr P. Heathfield, National Union Secretary, dated 9 and 12 March 1984.
    I am further instructed to ask you to support immediately a demand for the National Executive Committee to be recalled for the purpose of arranging an early national ballot of the membership.
    Finally, there is no reason why Saturday and Sunday, 24 and 25 March 1984, could not be used for a meeting of the National Executive Committee.

By 23 March, I had received a copy of a letter sent by Jim Colgan, General Secretary of the Midlands NUM, to both Arthur Scargill and Peter Heathfield, and a similar copy of his letter sent to all NUM Executive members, calling for a meeting and a national ballot vote. They had reached the point of miner fighting miner, he said, with members being prevented from going to work by pickets from other parts of the country and some of their own members who had voted to strike in the Midlands ballot.

A copy of a tele-message sent by Sid Vincent to Peter Heathfield was received on 24 March. It stated that the North Western area (Lancashire) at its conference had unanimously condemned the violent picketing, and, noting the ballot result in the Lancashire area, agreed to ask the NUM officials to call an immediate special NUM Executive meeting with a view to holding a national ballot. They would try to work normally but would not cross official picket lines.

On 26 March, I wrote yet again to Peter Heathfield and Arthur Scargill, quoting my previous letters and demanding a recall of the NUM Executive for the purpose of arranging a ballot vote. That same day, Henry Richardson confirmed with me by letter that his area, Nottinghamshire, had taken similar action.

Ted McKay also informed me that on 19 March he had written to Peter Heathfield asking for a meeting of the NUM Executive 'so that the national officials can take control of the situation nationally'.

What has become known as the 'secret public meeting' started with a telephone call on Monday, 26 March from the North Wales General Secretary, Ted McKay. It was a cloak-and-dagger operation, akin to something in a detective novel. But that morning triggered off a more sinister series of events and culminated in my becoming a target of violence.

'What are we going to do, Roy?' asked Ted. He was worried over how the union was being steered into conflict.

I told him to leave it to me and I'd get back. I phoned Sid Vincent. 'Don't you think we ought to do something and organize a meeting? I'm prepared to organize it if I can get enough people to agree.'

We discussed the possibilities, listed those who wanted a ballot and came up with:

Jack Jones	Leicestershire
Ken Toon	South Derbyshire
Ted McKay	North Wales
Ray Chadburn	Nottinghamshire
Trevor Bell	COSA
Denis Murphy	Northumberland
Harry Hanlon	Cumberland
Ron Dunn	Durham Mechanics
Harold Mitchell	Durham Area

And, of course, Sid Vincent and myself.

We wondered about the Midlands area – knowing that Jim Colgan, the area's comparatively new General Secretary, was a Scargill supporter.

'How about Joe McKie?' I asked. I was speaking of the Midlands President, a previous NEC member who had always defended the ballot vote. 'It might be better if we approach him for support, and he could tell us where the Midlands stands.' Sid agreed with me.

We decided to split the list down the middle and ring half each. Sid took Northumberland, Cumberland and Durham, and I took the rest.

My first call was to Jack Jones's office – but he wasn't available; he was in a council meeting upstairs, I was told. I asked the gentleman on the phone if he could get Jack out of the meeting. 'It is very important,' I said.

After a few minutes I heard: 'Hi ya, mate! What's the trouble?' It was Jack in his usual friendly manner. I explained the discussion I had had with Ted and Sid and asked him if he was agreeable to a meeting, and asked him if he could fix a room in his area, for it was a good central point. He thought a little. 'The Brant Inn on the A50 going into Leicester. We'll get in there.'

We were bound to attract publicity so he suggested we'd better have some police coverage 'just in case'. The picketing scenes had made us quickly realize that anyone who went against the strike could be in physical danger. Particularly just at that time, when feelings were running high.

I left the arrangements to him and he said we'd meet at the Inn next day at 2pm.

I replaced the receiver and sensed an air of excitement.

It looked as though this could be the start of a campaign within the NUM Executive to force a vote on a ballot for the members at last.

I telephoned Joe McKie and explained the aims. He said he'd like to join us, but there could be a backlash in his area.

'Where does the Midlands stand?' I asked. He told me they'd already voted more than 70 per cent against strike action and he personally was urging a national ballot. But he explained that it was better he didn't attend though he would personally back the ballot call.

I rang the others: Ken Toon, Ted McKay and Trevor Bell. I then confirmed with Sid Vincent the place and venue, and finally I rang Jack to say it was on.

'Trouble is, Jack,' I said, 'I can't get Ray Chadburn, and that means losing two votes from Nottinghamshire. I daren't ask Henry Richardson [the left-wing Secretary of Nottinghamshire], he may blow the gaffe.'

Jack explained that Ray was in the High Court attending a hearing about the pension fund, of which he was a trustee. After some discussion we came to the conclusion we had to make contact. Best method was to trust the NCB and telephone Ned Smith, the Board's Director General of Industrial Relations, to get word to Ray.

'Leave it with me,' he said.

It was 6pm when the telephone rang at home. It was Ray Chadburn.

'I got a message, Roy. What's up, what's it all about?' He was in a hotel room in London and I explained the situation.

Ray said he couldn't tell Henry Richardson and he couldn't leave London the next day because 'the others will suspect something'. He suggested I got in touch with the Nottinghamshire Financial Secretary, Roy Lynk. 'Tell him I told him to attend and pledge our two votes.'

He wished me the best of luck and said he'd see me at the next NUM Executive meeting.

By now it was becoming a strain. I was putting my head on the block and asking others to do the same. I telephoned Roy Lynk, and he said: 'I'll be there. Have no worry.'

I could visualize the headlines the next night in our local paper, the *Evening Sentinel*. I was excited at the prospect that at least something was being done to get the ballot vote back to the membership.

One further thing had to be done before going to bed that night. It had to be late, so that I knew there was no chance of arrangements being called off. I phoned Bob MacSporran, Power Group President, the only lay member of the union who would, I decided, be privy to the proposed meeting. I told him about our decision.

'You'll need endorsement by our Executive,' he said.

I replied: 'Our policy is for a ballot, and I am an NEC member. We shall have to tell them later and really I need no endorsement.'

'Alright,' he said, not too enthusiastically, 'but let me know what goes on.'

Next morning, 27 March, I went to my office in Hanley, dealt with the post and checked out the arrangements with Jack Jones. My mail contained a reply from NUM headquarters signed by the Assistant Secretary. It explained that Arthur Scargill was away from the office for two weeks involved in a High Court case, but would be given my letter of 26 March, on his return.

I set off for the meeting – hoping everyone else was doing the same. The fifty-odd miles didn't take long, and as I drove on to the hotel forecourt I saw a television camera crew.

I was full of mixed emotions, but knew I was doing the right thing for the men. When I got into the hotel, however, I began to fear the worst. A room did appear to be reserved but I couldn't find any other members of the Executive. I roamed about outside and began to panic a little.

Then came Trevor Bell. Gradually the others showed up but no one came from Durham or Northumberland.

Sid Vincent arrived, demanding somewhat irately who had arranged for the television crew to be present. 'I shall get bloody hung in my area.' He explained he had walked in, walked out, but had finally decided to come back again. We all pacified him.

The meeting began. They asked me to take notes and Jack Jones was made Chairman. Messages were received from Northumberland, Durham, and Durham craftsmen reporting that they would support a ballot vote demand, and apologizing for non-attendance. We knew that the cokemen too had registered a vote for a ballot. Then each area in turn signified their intention to get a ballot: Leicestershire, South Derbyshire, North Wales, Nottinghamshire (two votes), COSA, Lancashire, the Power Group, Cumberland, giving us thirteen votes – a majority. Although the Midlands area had not attended we were sure that they would make fourteen votes in total.

We had further discussions, reviewing the position of those who had voted in the areas, those who had not, and the whole situation in the coalfields. It was clear that all those present had written to head office demanding a recalled NUM Executive meeting with a view to implementing a national individual ballot vote. Trevor Bell handed copies of his letters to me with copies of a reply from Peter Heathfield saying they were monitoring the situation.

It was agreed that from the debate a statement be developed and a message be sent out from the meeting. I had taken the notes, so it was felt that I should draw up the statement. I moved to a separate table to rewrite the points, and Trevor Bell assisted me. I read it to them once, twice, three times, making minor amendments until it was acceptable to all.

I walked out to the waiting press men and declared: 'I am going to read you a statement; no additions, no questions. Right!'

The cameras turned and the pencils scribbled, and I read the statement:

Our purpose at this meeting is to achieve solidarity between us and to get a national ballot, being concerned as to the future of the union and, to achieve the unity that is so necessary. This can only be achieved by retaining the democracy of the ballot vote, the union being larger than us, the national officials, or any individual.

It is agreed unanimously that a message be sent out from this meeting to all members where a democratic vote has been taken not to strike, or where the members have been advised to continue working until a national ballot vote is taken, to endeavour to work normally whilst continuing to apply the overtime ban guidelines.

We are unanimously of the opinion that the national officials should recognize the validity of the democratic decisions taken in various areas and, whilst appreciating the right of areas to take strike action under Rule 41, they should also recognize the decision taken by other areas not to strike. We hope and trust that they will instruct accordingly.

Having made these points, and being concerned as to the future of the NUM and the industry, and reaffirming our commitment to it, we call upon the national officials, being in the knowledge that at least thirteen members out of twenty-four members of the National Executive Committee are in favour of a national ballot vote, to call an immediate meeting of the National Executive Committee towards organizing the taking of an immediate *national ballot vote*. We can then concentrate on bringing public attention to the real issues facing the union and the industry.

By the time I had finished, some of my colleagues were standing beside me and were also seen on camera. We quickly dispersed and I went back to Jack Jones's office in Coalville, where the statement was typed. I took a copy, and Jack circulated it to all others at the meeting and to NUM officials.

I drove home to Stoke, exhilarated but shattered. It was not to be peaceful evening. The telephone was hot with calls.

Among the callers was the BBC 'Newsnight' team.

'The meeting this afternoon – we would like you to appear tonight. Would you be prepared to travel to Nottingham studios? We'll send a car.'

I explained I'd only just got in from Leicester. It was a long way and I was tired.

They insisted, telling me that Jack Collins, the Kent area Secretary, would be in the London studios with an opposite view. That was enough. I agreed.

I gave as good as I got during the discussion later that night on television. I didn't personalize the issues as Jack did. But he certainly annoyed me when he called the Power Group 'a few drivers who are not miners'.

It had been a hard day. I told the taxi driver after the drive back to drop me half a mile from home. I would walk and get some air. It turned out much better than that. I started to walk and a voice came from the car park of the local pub. It was Ted Archer, the proprietor. 'Come over here, film star. You're earned a drink.'

I got home at 1am after Ted had rejuvenated me with two or three scotches.

Next day I was up early and off to the office for 8.30 am. About 9.30 the local reporter dealing with the strike, Peter Davis, phoned me and asked for comments on the reception committee I had outside. Up to then I hadn't even noticed anyone was there. I now looked through the windows and could see men at various points on the five-road junction outside my office. They were obviously waiting until some of them made the first approach to the office entrance. When some did, Harry Tilstone, our Finance Officer, telephoned the police.

The chants started outside. 'Ottey is a Tory,' I heard them jeer.

'Bring your book and pencil, Janice,' I told my secretary. 'Sit at my desk as usual. I shall agree to meet some of them. You make a note of what is said – that should have a calming influence on them.'

A man burst into the office, gesticulating madly and shouting, 'You fucking bastard!' and other obscenities. Though I was frightened, I was determined to remain calm.

Two other men burst in, shouting furiously and demanding that I met the jeering crowd outside.

A police inspector appeared in my office doorway. 'Mr Ottey, I need to know your intentions. Are you meeting these men outside?'

'I've told one of those who have left that I will meet a deputation of six of them,' I replied. 'That's all I am prepared to do. Will you ensure that only six of them get in?'

The inspector obviously did his job and six men came in, all trying to talk at once and looking as menacing as the previous ones. I noticed straightaway that only three were Power Group members – all branch officials – the other three being from the Midlands area.

I waited until they had almost exhausted themselves, and listened to them repeating their claims that I had created disunity by advising the men on television to return to work. This I could not understand since the statement had been most carefully worded to cover all prevailing situations in the various areas.

Finally, I handed each of the six a copy of the statement drawn up at the previous day's meeting and which I had read on television.

As they read, there was a noticeable change in attitude, culminating with their saying that it was different from what I said on television. Then one of them, Dave Kell, Branch Secretary at Wolstanton Colliery, said: 'They cut it off halfway, that's obvious.'

I sensed a degree of deflation now but, as they left, there was no doubt that more would be heard from them. Power Group policy was under attack, summed up by Dave Kell's words: 'We have started fighting already and we are not prepared to wait for a ballot any longer.' However, I was equally determined to uphold the policy. I spoke out in a statement printed in local newspapers:

I am not prepared to stand by and watch this great union of ours be destroyed by civil war. I warned there would be civil war if each area took their own action and sent in flying pickets, and this is what has happened. It is the beginning of the end for this union as a fighting force if we do not go forward as a united body. We have got to demonstrate forcefully to Mr Scargill and the General Secretary Mr Heathfield that miners want their democratic right: that is, a national ballot.

The members must unite to get a ballot, if needs be they must demonstrate in the streets. We are talking about democracy, which is something the vast majority of the men are prepared to fight for. We cannot afford to capitulate to the forces that are at work today and lose the right to a national vote. I believe there is no excuse for not reconvening the National Executive Committee over the next few days.

It seemed that the statement had some effect, for 350 miners defied pickets at a Staffordshire pit and demanded the right to work, while six members of the Power Group crossed picket lines at Silverdale Colliery, North Staffordshire, where I was due to attend a branch meeting the following Thursday. I had also received news from Sid Vincent saying that the men in his area, having been on strike for one week, were likely to return to work on Monday, 2 April.

Sid had sent a letter to Peter Heathfield saying: 'I have appealed to you . . . to call a Special National Executive Committee meeting in order to co-ordinate the present situation nationally, and I have failed. . . . I must now advise you that whatever happens in this area on Monday, 2 April 1984 the national officials will be responsible. I can't hold the members any longer.'

On Thursday morning, 29 March, I set off for Silverdale Colliery for the branch meeting, making sure to take my television statement, Power Group policy resolutions and, not least, letters received from branches in the North Staffordshire district, in which the members were demanding a ballot.

Arriving at the pit welfare club, a police mini-van was parked outside the entrance drive. I parked just inside the drive, got out and told the policemen (there were about eight of them) who I was and that they should keep an eye on me. 'Okay, we know who you are,' said one.

I then got back in the car, drove up to the club and parked. I could see the men waiting inside the club with their newly-painted, do-it-yourself placards, proclaiming, among other things, 'Ottey is a Tory,' and 'No ballot'. Other men stood by the door.

As I got out, there was complete pandemonium. The men inside rushed out to join the others waiting for me, chanting slogans.

It was a tense moment. The men were angry; some of them were spitting at me, but I knew that I must not show fear. I walked through them, saying 'Good morning' and catching hold of one of the placards as I went, my hands getting covered in white paint. Seeing the rostrum on stage from which I was to speak, I placed the placard on top of it. 'Ottey is a traitor,' it said.

The area around the bar was full, and many had been drinking for a while. The Power Group Branch President, Trevor Rushton, welcomed me and asked whether the Midlands area members drinking at the bar could stay inside whilst I addressed the meeting. 'No chance,' I replied, 'this is a properly convened Power Group branch meeting and only our members can attend.'

This decision made the lobbyists even angrier, and they kept up a barage of abuse, chanting slogans and trying to burst into the room through the entrance doors as I addressed the 200 or so members, explaining Power Group policy, our attempt to recall the NUM Executive and talking about the television statement.

Question-time followed, with those for and against expressing their views. It went on for about two hours. The Branch Secretary, Terry Carr, small but tough, concluded with a written speech, ending, 'I have tried it their way, being on strike to get a ballot. Now, I am going to try it my way: I am starting to work next Monday and shall keep going until there is a ballot.'

There was near-silence inside, but the noise outside was growing louder than ever and I wondered how I would be able to drive away. I shall always be grateful to the tall blond young Power Group member who said, 'Come on Roy, I shall see you out safely and ride with you.'

As we walked out through the chanting, spitting crowd, I felt dirty and degraded. My young friend waited whilst I paused to speak to some of them, climbed into the passenger seat and indicated another way out, thereby infuriating the lobbyists blocking the drive, who were denied their opportunity of kicking and thumping the car.

It should be pointed out that within weeks many of the lobbyists at this meeting were back at work, crossing picket lines which became smaller, while Terry Carr, was leading the fight for a national ballot, and consequently came into conflict with the Power Group Executive.

The Power Group Executive met on the following day and endorsed by actions in trying to achieve an NUM Executive meeting and a national ballot, and confirmed that the written statement I had made on television was in line with Power Group policy. They went on to say that they did not condone violence on picket lines, from whatever quarter it came, believing it to be counter-productive.

Their statement of support was not to prevent the activists on the left from exercising their vengeance, however, as we were soon to see at Keresley, Coventry.

The weekend preceding this event shook me further still. On the Saturday morning, whilst Doris and I were getting ready to go shopping, the doorbell rang.

A gentleman at the door introduced himself as being from the CID. He told Doris and me that letters had been received by them which indicated that we were in need of protection. 'What will you be doing over the weekend? Where will you be shopping in Hanley? What is the car number? Make sure you keep a watch around the house while you are in.'

Then a policeman arrived. 'He will be keeping a watch also!' the inspector went on. 'Phone if you are suspicious of anything. It would pay to put the burglar alarm on even at night when you are in bed. Don't get too concerned, but be careful for the next few days!'

They left and, although they had told us not to be too concerned, the Saturday morning shopping was done as if in a trance. How could people act in this way when all that I was doing was seeking the democratic rights of the membership, laid down by rules of the union, and fully endorsed by my own Executive? I was soon to realize that there were many who were not concerned with democracy.

Monday morning, 2 April, I got up early and set off to pick up Power Group President Bob MacSporran who was to accompany me to the Keresley branch committee meeting, just outside Coventry. The committee was split at Keresley, half continuing to work until a ballot vote was secured, and the other half, like so many in the industry, torn between the justice of their right to a ballot and their loyalty to the union by not crossing picket lines, and were in effect on strike.

We arrived at the colliery club, parked the car in the car park and walked to the entrance where, as usual, about a dozen to fifteen lobbyists were waiting, shouting, 'Scab!' and 'Traitor!' We walked past, through the large club room, and up the stairs to a small room where the meeting was to be held.

We talked, amicably though with feeling, for about two hours. It was obvious that there was to be no reconciliation of the views and stances adopted by the two factions. There would certainly be a continuation of disagreement, and over the ensuing weeks the whole village of Keresley was 'split' down the middle. There were many instances of intimidation and violence, and one Power Group member was sacked, accused of assaulting a working miner at the picket-lines.

The meeting came to a close, and we went downstairs to leave. The club room was full; there must have been about 200 men sitting there, drinking and talking.

As we reached the room, a group rose to their feet, glasses in hand. Led by a tall, heavy man, they blocked our path to the door, which was at the other end of the long room. At that moment it might just as well have been on the other side of the world.

The big man started to remonstrate about my television appearance, accusing me of telling the men to go back to work and poking me in the chest with his glass to emphasize each point. More men got to their feet and started to surround us, shouting constantly, the noise getting louder by the second. I tried to give some explanation. I knew it was useless; they were in no mood to listen.

My heart was thumping as I turned to Bob whose face was by now ashen-white. 'Come on Bob, let's move gently towards the door.' By now the men were waving their arms and glasses of beer, growing more and more menacing.

I got to where I thought the entrance door was and went through it. Immediately, I heard laughter behind me, and I only realized why when I found myself in the club kitchen!

Trying not to panic, I had to go back and face them again. I did so, rejoined Bob and edged towards the next door, the men pressing behind us. We went through into the daylight, walking quickly across the car park to the car.

'Bloody hell!' Bob and I said almost in unison, as we saw both front tyres had been deflated. We looked around: the men were coming through the doors, glasses in hands. It was apparent that they didn't intend us to make a quick get-away. The Branch Secretary, Malcolm Ward, was at the side of the car trying to engage us in conversation, completely oblivious, it seemed, of what might happen if we didn't get away.

'Get in the car!' Bob shouted. 'Lock 'em as well!' he said as we got in, slamming the doors.

'Drive off!' he shouted again.

My heart was thumping even louder as I drove off, wrestling with the steering wheel.

It was at least one and a half miles before we got to a motorway service station, and could stop and survey the tyres, which were by now smoking, with one tyre ruined and unusable.

We managed to fit the spare and inflate the other sufficiently to drive back slowly to Coalville. As Bob and I drove home we were in no doubt that we would have suffered some sort of assault if we hadn't got away.

On 4 April, with the new tyres fitted, Jim Dowling accompanied me to Haig Colliery in the Cumberland area. We attended a meeting, at which NCB proposals to reduce manpower, offering redundancy to those wishing to leave or transfer to other areas, were discussed. The workforce at this pit, in contrast to Silverdale and Keresley, had decided to continue working.

I had had a very busy few days and had witnessed some of the most frightening scenes in my career. But what was far more worrying still was that although the industry was in a turmoil and some areas had called for a Special NUM Executive meeting to discuss a ballot, there was no initiative towards securing peace in the coalfields from the NUM officials. Each day the crisis deepened and if Arthur Scargill and Co. wanted any convincing how deep the split in the union had become, the warnings soon to be sounded by some area leaders would leave them in no doubt.

– 5 –

Tension Grows

The next ordinary meeting of the NUM Executive was due to take place on Thursday, 12 April. The night before I received a telephone call from Joe Wills, President of the North Staffordshire district miners, asking if I would take a sealed letter from him and give it to Jim Colgan, their area General Secretary and a keen Scargill supporter, whom he had been trying to contact all day. The contents, he said, were an instruction to Jim Colgan to vote at the meeting for a national ballot.

Despite making arrangements to pick up the letter, misunderstandings occurred, and I didn't get it till next morning when Jim Dowling brought it. He was going to drive me to Sheffield for the meeting, being larger than me and better able to look after the car and me at what we suspected would be a heavily lobbied meeting.

Our suspicions proved correct. When we arrived at the car park entrance, which is in the basement of NUM headquarters, television camera crews and police almost prevented entry. But Jim drove through, parked, and together we walked up the steps and slipped through the glass doors of the building.

The police had kept the entrance clear and although we were aware that a very large crowd of lobbyists were present, the scale of the scene was not appreciated until the members of the NUM Executive started to assemble in the lounge outside the Executive conference room and looked through the windows at the masses of lobbyists and police eleven floors below.

People were cheering, jeering, singing and shouting, swaying and pushing at the police lines. The atmosphere both in and outside the building was tense.

I handed the letter from Joe Wills to Jim Colgan, telling him that it related to how he should vote, and we all moved into the conference room.

Arthur Scargill came in and called the meeting to order. Having opened the meeting, there was immediate intervention from Owen Briscoe, General Secretary, Yorkshire area, who proposed that the meeting should be adjourned until the police in the street outside had been removed.

After what had happened to me the previous week, I thought how foolish it would be to leave us defenceless. I had already pointed this out to Roger Windsor, Chief Executive Officer, who had been about to suggest the removal of the police prior to the meeting. I think he had changed his mind when I told him about our experience in Coventry. Also, of course, a possible result of Owen Briscoe's proposal might have been to stop a ballot vote being taken.

Arthur Scargill started to say he had a suggestion to make, but he was interrupted by Denis Murphy, Northumberland General Secretary, who said he had phoned head office prior to the meeting asking for the venue to be changed 'because somebody could get killed'.

Arthur then said there had already been a number of arrests outside and if the venue had been switched it could have been a lot worse.

I was just anxious for the meeting to start, hoping that we would achieve a ballot vote decision. I was wondering too about the information whispered in my ear by a member of staff that Jim Colgan had been at head office all the previous day. No wonder Joe Wills hadn't been able to contact him!

Ray Chadburn, President, Nottinghamshire area, started to say that he was not at all pleased with the police and that Nottinghamshire had become an island. Arthur Scargill cut him off to say again he had a suggestion to make and that he had never seen anything like the scenes outside.

I was not surprised at any of the scenes outside, given his statement reported in the *Morning Star* some days previously on 28 March:

> To defeat them [the Tories] it will take people and cash on a mammoth scale. Every sinew in every factory, office, dole queue, docks, railway, plant and mill will need to be strained to the maximum. Waiting in the wings are four million unemployed whose numbers could swell the picket lines at any time. . . .
>
> What is urgently needed is the rapid and total mobilisation of the trade union and Labour movement to take positive advantage of the unique opportunity to defend our class and roll back the machinery of oppression, exploitation and deep-seated human misery.

Arthur spoke again. The three NUM officials had had a discussion and were suggesting that all items on the agenda except the situation in the industry be left until another meeting.

Jack Jones from Leicestershire, a real stalwart of the right, afraid of nothing and no one, angrily disagreed, saying it was the responsibility of the NUM Executive to deal with the business before them. 'To do any other,' he continued, 'shows that we are succumbing to what is happening outside.'

That really provoked George Rees, sitting beside me, and in a voice charged with emotion, he said: 'I never thought I would see the day when we had a meeting like today's.' His voice rising to a higher pitch, he shouted. 'Some people scream about Poland. Call yourself trade unionists, you don't know the meaning of the word! I am moving that we deal with the minutes and leave the meeting until the police have left.'

Trevor Bell, from COSA, was even more angry and, glaring across the tables, he retorted: 'Let's not forget that the buses have been paid for. It is organized, and the police wouldn't be there if the lobbyists were not!'

It was a good point and obviously struck home to those who had done the organizing of the mass lobby.

Arthur again intervened. 'I am suggesting again that we discuss the minutes and then the situation in the areas and let our lads [outside] get away. Does the meeting agree.'

George Rees shouted, 'No,' which triggered emotional outbursts from all sides of the tables, which were set in a rectangle with the two ends at least 30 feet apart. You had to shout if like me and George Rees you were sitting at the opposite end to the Chairman, Arthur Scargill.

Arthur now had no alternative. He put the question to the vote, and this resulted in thirteen votes to ten in favour of the meeting continuing as the President had suggested.

The atmosphere became a little less tense as we progressed through the minutes of the last meeting. There were questions raised and answered about union funds and steps that had been taken at the previous meeting to try and protect them, but nothing was divulged as to what exactly these actions were.

Tension mounted again when suddenly it was noticed through the huge 40-feet picture windows that on a roof-top opposite a camera crew was setting up their gear, apparently in an attempt to film and record the proceedings of the meeting. It was decided to take the precaution of drawing all the curtains on that side of the room.

When this was done and everyone was quiet again, Arthur said: 'I have made no statement on the situation, and what I would like to do is to advise on procedure.'

He went on to relate the content of National Conference decisions and resolutions, the NUM Executive agreement to a Special Delegate Conference in October 1983 and all consequent decisions up to 8 March 1984 when the Executive had agreed to sanction the strike action in Yorkshire and Scotland.

He then stated that the Executive had rejected the ballot vote proposed by Trevor Bell on 8 March and said, 'I am going to allow a wide-ranging discussion and I hope you don't put me in a position of having to rule.'

At this stage I sensed I should be extra alert to any devious moves, but Jack Jones was quickly into the fray. 'I have a good memory,' he said. 'There was not a resolution put to the vote at the NEC on 8 March, on the ballot.'

He said the Executive sanctioned Scotland and Yorkshire areas and, any other area which agreed but did not give sanction to invade other areas with intimidation and mass-picketing.

'It is a tragic situation of miner against miner and a position in some areas that the men would go to work if they were not prevented,' he added.

Jack Taylor from Yorkshire forcefully interjected and challenged him to prove his statement about Yorkshire, but Jack Jones was not to be put off. 'I did not mention areas by name,' he said, 'but there are areas in that position. Democracy works both ways, our membership is split. Not 80 per cent to 20 per cent but more than that. In fact, our area was forced to have a vote and it resulted in 89.17 per cent against striking.

'If there had been a national vote, it would have prevented that and I say to those who go to the media and say we should not have a vote, there is only one rule book and it is sacrosanct.'

The President, Arthur Scargill, was the guardian of the rules and they could only be changed by the will of the members at conference, he said. There was only one way to unite and that was by holding a national ballot vote of all members. Those who said there shouldn't be a ballot were afraid to face the members. 'You know we've got some strange bedfellows,' he said.

Jack Jones then stood up to his full height of nearly six feet, draped over the green cloth-covered table for all to see a big advert from the *Guardian*, and said dramatically: 'Ken Livingstone says we should all have a vote.' (This was, of course, the advert with the slogan 'SAY NO TO NO SAY' used by Ken Livingstone in his fight to prevent the abolition of the GLC.)

At this, there were shouts of derision from around the tables, especially from the anti-ballot faction. Arthur Scargill tried to restore order but, in any case, it was obvious that Jack Jones was not going to be stopped again.

'It is a tragic day that we are in,' he continued. 'I speak to many in other areas and they see it as a political strike. We have lost sight of the cause. There are people who have infiltrated picket lines who are not in favour of the TUC, the Labour Party or the miners. We have not got a national strike. Head office phones every day to my office to discuss the situation and I deplore the fact that this happens because they [head office] are only serving one part of the membership [the strikers]. The battle has to be fought and won, but we shall only get that with the support of the members.'

Jack then lifted from the table a letter which he had sent to

Peter Heathfield, and read it. Briefly, it said, 'This National Executive Committee of the NUM, recognizing the continuing divisions within the membership, agrees that a national ballot vote be held.'

He then proposed formally that such a ballot be held over pit closures.

Jack Taylor from Yorkshire couldn't resist getting in next and certainly indicated his attitude to ballots. 'I am surprised,' he said, 'a ballot vote is a luxury we cannot afford.'

He carried on, 'I shall have to go to Cortonwood and tell them the pit is closed. We are not getting into a position where one man votes another out of his job. We shan't have a union if we go like that. We have tried to get the policies you [Jack Jones] have laid down implemented. We all go to the rostrum at Conference and it is all written down saying what we are going to do. You can't back off now. We have a big area now prepared to fight.'

He said MacGregor had stopped attacking union funds, but added: 'They can take all our money but we shall remain in business and you are living in cloud cuckoo land if you did not think we would come to you for support.'

This was a reference to the fact that Yorkshire, immediately their strike had been sanctioned on 8 March, sent their flying pickets over the borders into other mining counties.

However, Jack Taylor went on, 'We had a bloke killed, and it was the hardest day for me to go to that funeral. I want to be a democrat but in Yorkshire we are not going to have democracy abused.'

He said of course it was a political strike. If the Labour Party were in power, the NUM would not be in this position. 'We either take MacGregor on or accept. The unity we want is the miners standing together. I never thought I would see leaders taking men across picket lines saying we will fight our way in.'

This, again, was a reference to Jack Jones, for it had been alleged that he had made that statement in his own Leicestershire area.

There then followed what I considered to be the most emotional speech of the meeting, particularly as it came from a left-winger, Henry Richardson. He said, 'The tragedy is in what Jack Taylor is saying. The members in Notts have tried everything and we are failing all along the line. There are 20,000 from 27,000 who have said "No" and we here can't forget what is happening. The longer we go on the bigger the split. Our men who are striking are getting nothing.' He said in Cresswell village there had been daubing of doors and smashing of windows. Men in the village were crying.

'Aren't they [the men] going to lose faith? It is no use saying it is a mistake because you are only making the situation worse. The majority of Notts miners are saying "We shall not move without a ballot." '

He said if Yorkshire and Scotland wanted to strike then let them. But Notts said 'No' unless there was a ballot and the men had a say. There had been many pickets throwing bricks. He said he had lived in the village all his life and the union had lost all support in one hour.

In an even more emotional cry, Henry went on: 'I would hope we have a ballot. If we lose,' he questioned, 'are we in any different position to now? We are destroying trade unionism in Nottinghamshire.' He said Nottinghamshire men were saying 'The more they come, the more determined we shall be.'

With that sort of speech within the NUM Executive from a left-wing Executive member, how could Arthur Scargill say, as reported in *The Times* on 2 July 1984:

> Mr MacGregor is talking nonsense [about the intimidation of non-striking miners and their families] and he has no evidence to back that statement up. . . . I will not accept that my members have been in any way involved in intimidation. My facts show me quite clearly that the people guilty of intimidation and violence in this dispute have been the police.

My long-time friend and colleague Ken Toon, whose area (South Derbyshire) had voted against strike action, then said: 'There are no divisions on this NEC but the men [the members] have ripped each other apart.'

He went on and seconded the proposal made by Jack Jones on the call for a national ballot, referring also to the overtime ban and the magnificent support given by the men. 'The problem is,' he said, 'the sanctioning of the Yorkshire and Scottish action. I have sympathy, but it was granted under Rule 41. The other areas were invited to support and I put over the policy but my area insisted on a vote.

'The ballot was "Are you prepared to support Yorkshire and Scotland against MacGregor's closures" and the men voted against it. The NEC now has to take a decision,' he said. 'I shall defend my people. They are not scabs. Rule 41 was agreed at the last meeting, but it is an area problem. No area has the right to impose their will on another area.'

Ken went on to refer to the resolution of Annual Conference which opposed pit closures and manpower losses but which also said that a ballot vote of the members should be taken at 'an appropriate time'.

'It is now the appropriate time,' he said. 'I think we would get 55 per cent and, if we did, South Derbyshire would stand by it. I agree with Henry Richardson – if we lose it would not be any worse than now. Rule 41 is not right. We should be careful how we start a National Strike.'

In his usual explosive way, Eric Clarke, General Secretary for Scotland, said he was disgusted with statements that had been made in the media: 'You are being used. The media does not want us for democracy and I oppose cameras being in at ballot counts.' He said intimidation worked both ways and claimed lads had been kicked and arrested. There had been a whole army of police facing them. 'Stop calling our men,' he shouted. 'They are being intimidated by the police. Do you think if the ballot is no strike that the men are going to accept at Bogside, Polmaise and Kent?' He said he was protecting his members' interests. Britain was heading for a police state and the police were defying Parliament, he claimed. MacGregor was the hit man and a political appointment. And there was a gut reaction from the miners.

'The media will decry us. I went to the funeral [of the boy who died in Nottinghamshire] but many of the NEC were not there. It [the pit closures] will not go away in Nottinghamshire with a ballot vote. It [the ballot] is not wanted for democracy. Some of you voted for action in Scotland and Yorkshire and I hope you are all humiliated by the support we get from other unions.'

He then referred to one newspaper, the *Daily Express*, calling for a ballot vote and said, 'Scotland are not going down that road.'

He went on, 'On the incentive agreement, you did it then by Rule 41. We did organize our men to be here today. They are united. They are our future. Not Jack Jones but Jack Taylor.'

What Eric didn't say was that although Rule 41 was used for the implementation of the incentive scheme in various areas, there were no pickets sent into other areas to enforce its adoption. Rather, the men in the other areas forced their officials to introduce it because they wanted the benefits.

Idwal Morgan, General Secretary of the Cokemen's area, as we had been informed at the caucus right-wing meeting in Leicester, had been instructed to vote for a ballot by his area.

'I am not proud of my mandate,' he said, and added the only way they would get unity was by attacking MacGregor's closure plan. 'I am voting against my conscience and I will be ashamed.'

Trevor Bell, with whom Ted McKay and I had voted on 8 March against sanctioning strikes in Scotland and Yorkshire, then said COSA had had both a conference and a delegate meeting.

He said his members in Yorkshire were pleased, but they were broke because of the strike. He was getting many letters and pressures were building up to the point where the sacrifices throughout the NUM were uneven.

Trevor said it was time everyone had the opportunity to say whether they wanted to make the sacrifice. Despite predictions by some, pits had not collapsed like falling dominoes.

'In fact,' he argued, 'even where they voted for strike, men are going back to work. Nothing could damage the union more than what has happened since the last NUM Executive meeting. The NUM have been held up in the past as a model by the TUC against Tebbit [because of its democratic method of balloting members]. We need a more effective NUM.'

He said he had noted what Arthur Scargill had said about him ruling a ballot proposition out of order but there was no mention in the minutes of 8 March about a ballot vote. Today there was a proposal from Jack Jones under Rule 43, not Rule 41 as at the previous meetings. A Conference appeal would be on the issue of the decision on Rule 41.

Trevor was correct. Although the rules permit any area to appeal at Conference against any NUM Executive decision, there could be no appeal on the ballot vote proposal because a vote had not been taken at the meeting, and therefore not recorded.

It was now the turn of Jim Colgan, whose area headquarters in the Midlands were only some twenty miles from my own and, therefore, whose members were influenced by what I might say and vice-versa.

Jim said the 8 March decision told him he was in the midst of battle. The Midlands Executive supported the decision to back Yorkshire and Scotland. They had an area ballot which was 73 per cent against strike action but he added: 'The following week the Area Council overwhelmingly overturned the ballot result.'

What an admission of anti-democratic action! How could they perpetrate it on the men? They pleaded it was to protect the working men from the violence of the picket lines.

Looking down the table at me he said: 'I am ashamed of you, Roy Ottey, and your comrades because you destroyed the unity of our area.'

He referred to 1,800 policemen being on duty at one Midland pit in Warwickshire and accused them of intimidation.

'Roy Ottey destroyed the will of our men,' he said, pointing at me. 'You told the men to demonstrate for a ballot, even in the streets.'

He said he had had full instructions from his Executive to come to the meeting today and listen. He went on: 'My gut is telling me to bugger my area. The fight is to do with Mac-Gregor. If we can't stand together we shall fail. I shall be asking for a national ballot. But, if it hadn't been for the caucus [the "secret public meeting"] in Leicester, we would have had more men out.'

I didn't mind one bit that Jim pointed his accusations at me.

He was only demonstrating that I obviously held more sway with his members than he did.

Sid Vincent was to demonstrate the attitude of the men in his area and, indeed, many others.

Sid said if he did not vote for a ballot, there would be a funeral in his area. He meant his own, and some members laughed at this. He had to vote for a ballot if Arthur Scargill did not rule against one.

'I even agreed that a Yorkshire delegate addressed our conference in Lancashire. But the delegates still voted to work,' he said.

Arthur Scargill should really have ruled here that an individual ballot vote would be taken. But Peter Heathfield, the union's General Secretary, quickly demonstrated that the NUM officials had other ideas.

'The debate that has taken place reflects the situation,' he said. 'There has been no change to indicate that it was necessary to call the National Executive meeting. I am not satisfied that a ballot will resolve the position.'

He said that after the 'secret public meeting' when Trevor Bell made a statement and I read a statement on television, men in North Derbyshire were ringing him and saying Ken Toon was driving men over picket lines in NCB vans and Ted McKay in North Wales was doing the same.

'It is important that we listen to the lads at a Special Delegate Conference. We don't want a ballot vote. Democracy is not about voting another man out of a job. We should not be going up that path,' he said.

So that was the idea! No national ballot – a Conference instead. How could Peter Heathfield say we didn't want a ballot? 'Voting another man out of a job' was the way Jack Collins from Kent had put it when we appeared on the television programme 'Newsnight'. But both he and all the other anti-ballot activists were using the exact opposite ploy by addressing the miners with the words 'Nobody's job is safe'.

Well, they couldn't have it both ways. If nobody's job is safe, then they should all be entitled to vote.

George Rees said: 'It is hypocrisy hiding behind a ballot. In

1982 Jack Jones and Ted McKay went to the rostrum at Annual Conference to support industrial action on the Vale of Belvoir.

'Many of you speak against Tebbit but then turn your backs on action. Two pits were closed in South Wales last year and we have been out four weeks now. National ballots are loaded against us and all of you are against us. It makes me sick.'

I felt sick too, so obvious was it that this dictatorial attitude went against the members' rights within the rule book and Annual Conference decisions.

Mick McGahey was next to speak. He said most men had voted with their feet. 'They are on strike and I warn you, it is the media who have got "ballotitis". It was war from the moment MacGregor was appointed. Those who met in Leicester should be ashamed of it. Nobody in here is against ballots, in fact a Special Conference should consider a ballot vote. You can express an opinion there. We need a conference to unify us.'

Mick referred to statements that miner was against miner but claimed: 'It is not like that in Scotland, Yorkshire or Kent. We must give serious consideration to a national ballot at a Special Conference,' he added.

I didn't feel the least bit ashamed about the Leicester meeting, but Mick should have been ashamed even to suggest that a conference would unify.

We knew perfectly well that the voting strength at Conference, dominated by the left-wing areas, would not favour a ballot vote decision. It was simply another deliberate move to prevent members exercising their long-held democratic rights.

Ted McKay, who was later in the year to be under such pressure from militants in North Wales that he and his family had to leave home and move to a secret address, then said that a ballot had been held in his area at which the policy of the union had been put forward but pickets' actions had deterred men from supporting the policy. As a result they had one pit at work and one pit out – North Wales only having two pits. 'What are we divided on?' he asked. 'Not the issue, just the tactics.'

He went on to say there was a serious division and that a fixed position at today's meeting would divide the NUM Executive even further. 'We have got to bridge the situation. And let me say this, I did not go to Leicester secretly; I went through the front door.'

Bill Stobbs said: 'Durham area is to be hit the most and we don't want anybody to vote on our jobs. I am mandated to vote for a one-day conference. If we don't have a conference the Board will have a right to close us.'

What Bill was really saying was that if we had a ballot and the men didn't vote for strike action, the NCB would think that they had the right to close pits. Presumably, therefore, the intention was not to let the men have a vote, but instead have a conference where member would vote against a ballot anyway.

'This annual confrontation is appalling,' said Denis Murphy, from Northumberland. He explained how they had had a branch ballot which was 90 per cent against the strike but they had subsequently turned the vote into a 52 per cent in favour of strike, by persuading members to think again.

He said he was 100 per cent in favour of the union's policy against pit closures, but was mandated to vote for a ballot because his members were sure they would get the right result.

'We cannot afford to lose it,' he said. 'It will be a life-long scar, you should all read what they did to us in 1926,' he added.

I had no need to: the memories of 1926 and after came back to me with a rush. However, I was abruptly brought back to the present when Wesley Chambers started to speak about Kent.

'Nobody is denying a ballot – it is just [a case of] when.' He said many other unions were supporting the NUM and they too were afraid what would happen if they lost the fight. The NCB, he claimed, would 'pick off' [i.e. close] Nottinghamshire's pits in due course but, he continued: 'Kent has lost its steel market, and the men of Kent have voted with their feet; it is only the media that are screaming "ballot".'

Stocky, red-faced Ray Chadburn from Nottinghamshire was next: and in his usual forceful manner said he had backed Arthur Scargill to get support at ten pits in the Nottingham-shire area, but they had failed.

'I got kicked by the Scots and Yorkshire men at the last [NEC] meeting' he said, and added that since 1 November, when the overtime ban started, thousands of men in Nottinghamshire had not had a full week's wages. About 20,000 were working, he said, and more and more of them were now saying, 'How can we get out of this union?'

Ray said: 'I don't want Spencerism*, but the men want a ballot.'

He went on, with emotion in his voice, to tell us of the way that some men were picketing his house and shouting: 'Come out here, you bastard!'

Added Ray: 'Miner is against miner and father against son, family against family.'

It was chilling to hear Ray describing the civil war that was taking place in his area.

With even more emotion, and looking across at some left-wing members, he said that in Nottinghamshire they had got Scots, Northumbrians and Welshmen, all of whom had been transferred from those areas when the pits had closed. The men were saying: 'Where were Clarke and McGahey [both from Scotland] when they closed our pits?'

Ray went on: 'We called them out on strike for two days and ordered them not to cross picket lines, but they still did and how can I stop them?'

He explained that he had been to see the 'fascist' policeman, the chief constable, about the police actions. 'I wish I were President in Scotland or Yorkshire. I have got 60 per cent transferees from other areas. The members have called for a secret ballot.'

The smart and moustachioed Gilbert Butler, whose area, North Derbyshire, had held a ballot, the members voting just over 50 per cent against strike action, asked accusingly: 'How about Jack Jones who said "If you want war you can have war"?'

Jack had indeed been reported to have said this to pickets. Then Gilbert turned to Ken Toon of South Derbyshire claiming that Ken had been at the picket lines advising his members to cross them, and he should be ashamed.

*George Spencer was the moderate Labour MP who led the miners in Nottinghamshire in 1926 to form a separate union, considered by many to be a bosses' union, and which in due course failed.

'A ballot vote will take us nowhere,' said Gilbert Butler. 'You should tell the men not to cross when the police are there.'

Henry Richardson suddenly shouted: 'We have!'

But Gilbert Butler went on: 'If this NEC said "All out", they would be. It would galvanize the men.'

The atmosphere began to get more tense with tempers fraying under the pressure of accusations. Owen Briscoe became really provocative, and interjected: 'Did Woodrow Wyatt* chair the meeting in Leicester?'

Sid Vincent reacted even more angrily and shouted: 'It is time we respected each other.' Referring to the left-wing caucus meetings he said: 'You meet regular.'

But Owen Briscoe went on saying that Nottinghamshire were the real hard core and, again, provocatively: 'I know what Spencerism is. Have you told your members about being sent home during the overtime ban?' Richardson and Chadburn said they had.

Then in what was a blatant demonstration that Yorkshire were set on doing their own thing – something they were accusing the anti-strike areas of doing – Briscoe said: 'If Yorkshire gets 55 per cent in a [national] ballot, don't think we shall go back to work. There is no call from the members for a ballot. We have only got one winder who has gone to work. We get letters of threats but a national ballot will serve no useful purpose.'

Big, tough Ron Dunn from the Durham craftsmen immediately got in: 'We should have a ballot for strike action.'

Johnny Weaver, from Yorkshire, then wondered where we were going when Jack Jones from Leicestershire had stated that areas had no right to picket other areas. He added that there had been 700 arrests in Yorkshire and they were carrying out the policies of the union.

Now it was my turn to speak. I referred to the Power Group's position and said that I had reported to my Executive but that we had decided not to have a ballot – the reason being that we believed there should be a national ballot vote within the rules. Also, our membership overlapped with other areas which could place individual members in a difficult situation, if our ballot

* The Labour MP considered by the left to be very right-wing.

contradicted the result of another area.

In North Staffordshire, I said, most men were on strike, but some were crossing picket lines. In Leicestershire, we only had our President, Bob MacSporran, and five others on strike. 'I simply want to say,' I said, 'that I certainly went through the front door at the Leicester meeting and, I tell you, Jim Colgan, just as you are voting for your area mandate, so am I for a ballot.'

Abe Moffat, representing the Scottish Craftsmen's Association, said the industry could no longer exist if the union did not fight. But there were some who did not want to fight MacGregor and his closures.

'You should have fire in your belly and call out your members,' he said. 'Other unions are supporting us – let's have unity.'

Emlyn Williams of South Wales, an excellent speaker, said the record of the union was good on democracy. He claimed that 2 April had seen Ted McKay of North Wales acting as a newspaper boy and crossing picket lines.

He added: 'To hide behind a ballot is cowardice. Our coalfields will stay out on strike,' and finished by saying that South Wales were going for broke.

I never really knew what he meant by this, and didn't question it, not directly anyway. But did he mean breaking the members, the South Wales NUM or what? More importantly, he certainly did not intend asking the members whether they agreed with such a course of action.

Arthur Scargill decided now was the time for him to speak. 'It is most crucial . . .' he started. 'Twenty-four have been arrested now and to say that five have gone to hospital would not be wide of the mark.'

He was referring to the lobbyists outside who were singing, cheering and chanting – an emotional disturbance which I am sure influenced all present.

He said the issue before us presented a problem for the trade union movement. Thatcher saw it that way through MacGregor, he said. Listening to the debate had exposed the weaknesses. There was 80 per cent on strike, and the transport unions had demonstrated their solidarity.

Arthur Scargill said the NUM had received two injunctions and, in line with the policy of the union and the TUC, these had been put in the dustbin.

He went on to explain that the Central Electricity Generating Board had spent £15 million to generate power with alternative fuels, all sanctioned by the Government. 'I have been handed secret documents on the stock position and there is only nine weeks' supply; in the steel industry there is only one and a half weeks', and there is an industrial crisis on stocks.'

Arthur seemed to love talking about secret documents which had been 'leaked' to him, all of which were described as 'devastating'. Not surprising, I suppose. After all, he didn't agree with secret dealings: everything should be in the open; he had said so in his first presidential address.

This particular 'leak' does not appear to have been reliable, though, if the statement made at the end of December 1984 by Peter Walker, Energy Minister, is to be believed: he said there would be no power cuts during the whole of 1985, and coal-burning would be increased at power stations.

However, Arthur then made the most profound statement so far: 'The decision you take today could spell the outcome of the future of this union.'

As I write in January 1985, the NUM is in a shambles, a direct result, I believe, of not having a ballot.

He went on to say that at the last NUM Executive meeting, after an excellent debate, Trevor Bell proposed a ballot vote. But, said Arthur, there was an amendment with twenty-one votes to three against Rule 43 being applied. Rule 30 (which says that any area 'aggrieved' by any decision of the NUM Executive shall have the right to appeal to the Conference), he said, was the only way a challenge could be made to that decision, and that would have to be at Annual Conference. But then he said a Special Conference could direct a ballot vote, and he suggested that proposals made today could go on the Special Conference agenda.

It was quite obvious to me that all these moves had been carefully planned beforehand. But, of course, the ordinary miner at the pits knew nothing about the way the strike was being organized behind the scenes. After all, wasn't it Arthur who told them that there would be no secrets as far as his leadership was concerned?

But back to the plot. 'If you are serious about ballot votes,' said Arthur, 'you should change the rule to a simple majority because you have 18,000 votes to overturn for a start. You could be in the same situation as NACODS, but you have an obligation to do something to get a majority.'

At that time the NUM needed 55 per cent for a strike. The NACODS situation was similar for, although their ballot had been over 50 per cent for strike action, the percentage was not high enough within the rules to call a strike.

Arthur said if a Special Conference agreed then a ballot vote would apply. A Special Delegate Conference had the right to be reconvened, he said.

'You must recognize my dilemma! I shall have to rule against a motion that need not be put.' Arthur was referring to the proposals made by Jack Jones for a ballot to be held over pit closures, which had been seconded by Ken Toon.

However, he then read through the decisions that had been taken on 8 March and a proposition that could be placed before a Special Delegate Conference to be held on 19 April – a date obviously decided prior to the meeting – reaffirming opposition to pit closures and calling for talks with the NCB which he said they (the NCB) had ended.

'You will then have unity,' said Arthur.

But there wasn't much unity in the meeting after a statement like that. It was like flashing the proverbial red rag at a bull. Denis Murphy shouted immediately: 'No way am I in a position to do any other than vote for a ballot.'

I backed Denis up: 'I must vote for nothing but a ballot.'

Sid Vincent also shouted: 'You will be in the same situation at the Special Delegate Conference.'

Arthur retaliated: 'But *you* won't, you will have a change of rule to a simple majority.'

Speaking up above the voices, Jack Jones said: 'I reserve my position. I want that right.'

Arthur, in a voice obviously meant to have a calming effect, said: 'I am in a constitutional position which is very difficult. You will have a right to discuss a ballot vote at a Special Conference.'

At this, Henry Richardson retorted: 'We are in a difficult position. We will just alienate the members more.'

Arthur went on: 'If I have to rule, you will have the status quo.' I took this to mean that we would carry on as we were and he would not allow a vote on a ballot at this meeting.

There was discussion across the tables. It was all very chaotic. Everyone was animated, and Arthur finally announced: 'I will have to rule the proposition of Jack Jones out of order.'

Another sign of what the left wing were up to emerged at that point. It seemed a bit tricky to me.

Idwal Morgan, the cokemen's leader, said: 'I shall have to vote for the ballot if you do not rule out of order now.'

Intrigue was implicit in this statement. Idwal was wanting to be released from his area mandate so he would not have to vote for a ballot.

Trevor Bell asked: 'On what basis will a Special Delegate Conference be held? A card vote will be stacked against a ballot vote.'

Denis Murphy, speaking primarily to Arthur, said: 'Use your common sense. I want a rule change, but I shall be hung from the nearest lamp-post if I don't vote for a ballot.'

Having reserved his position, Jack Jones did not intend to be thwarted. He stood up behind the table for greater impact and said: 'The union is greater than us, the President or the areas. I am mandated. It is all causing confusion. The President is talking a load of codswallop!'

Jack said the rule was clear and the NUM Executive was empowered to call a ballot.

There were shouts of interruption at that stage: some were derisive, but Jack refused to be intimidated. He said the Executive had a responsibility to decide today. He was not going to be deterred from his fight for a ballot.

'The President is in no constitutional difficulty,' said Jack. 'His only problem is that he is not capable of upholding the constitutional position.'

Jack said there would be more problems with men trying to go back to work if there was no ballot and the Executive had got to stop dallying. There had been no NUM Executive meetings since the last ordinary meeting on 8 March and that was not enough, he concluded.

There followed angry outbursts around the tables and Owen Briscoe fanned the flames when he said: 'The trouble is, there are too many NEC members committed to Thatcher.'

Denis Murphy asked what all the rush was about. 'Why have we got to have shotgun decisions?'

In the hubbub, Arthur Scargill said he wished to adjourn the meeting for fifteen minutes.

Immediately, the left and right groups banded together. I walked around the table to the opposite side, and joined Trevor Bell, Ted McKay, Jack Jones, Ken Toon and others.

It was my contention that we should all vote against the holding of a Special Delegate Conference, for I believed that the NUM Executive had the right to decide on a ballot vote.

However, in the time available, we agreed, almost talking in whispers, that we would challenge the President's ruling if he ruled the ballot vote proposal made by Jack Jones out of order. It was also decided that the President should be questioned as to how he could move an amendment to a resolution which was out of order.

Eventually, the meeting came to order and resumed, Arthur circulating a statement and a proposed amendment to Rule 43 on the ballot majority – in effect, changing the rule from requiring a 55 per cent majority for strike action to a simple majority. He went on to suggest that the documents, if accepted with the amendment to Rule 43, would resolve the problem.

Jack Jones and Denis Murphy immediately started shouting. They argued that Jack Jones's resolution for a ballot had been formally moved.

Again there was cross-talk, shouting and confusion. Then Arthur Scargill, in what I considered to have been an obviously predetermined decision, ruled Jack Jones's motion out of order on the grounds that at the last meeting on 8 March Trevor Bell had moved a motion on the ballot vote which had been seconded by me, and the only challenge that could be made to that NUM Executive decision was at Annual Conference.

This was ridiculous. The Trevor Bell motion was not even minuted. But Arthur was the President, and therefore in charge of the rules.

Henry Richardson, a left-winger, but mindful, it was apparent, of his Nottinghamshire mandate to go for a ballot, then attempted to persuade Scargill, by saying: 'The changed circumstances entitle us to support a ballot vote motion.'

To which Mick McGahey, sensing that difficulties were arising when left-wingers were wanting to vote for a ballot, spoke at length, and, in effect, said that unity could be got at the Special Conference.

Arthur could hardly wait for him to finish, and promptly ruled that a Special Delegate Conference would be held. Just as promptly, Jack Jones challenged the ruling.

Ray Chadburn was now shouting: 'Show us the rule, Chairman,' but, with arguments flowing to and fro, Arthur moved from the Chair, following the challenge to his ruling.

As required, Mick, without any comment, put the challenge to the Chairman's ruling to the meeting. The vote was thirteen to eight upholding the ruling.

Idwal Morgan then started to argue for a recommendation from the Executive for a ballot vote to be placed before the Special Conference. His action revealed the whole ploy of the left, for it was crystal-clear that both Idwal Morgan and Jim Colgan had been saved from contravening their area mandates. They had simply voted to uphold the Chairman's ruling.

Despite all the effort expended to organize the ballot vote at the Leicester meeting, we had been routed. No adjective can describe my feelings at that moment. I certainly felt exhausted and, to a great degree, bewildered that so many would go to what seemed almost any length to make sure the individual miner did not exercise his opinion.

Certainly, I could not contemplate the Special Delegate Conference upholding the right to a ballot vote: the meeting would continue to argue that the miners were 'voting with their feet' and going to strike anyway.

Arthur Scargill was back in the Chair and he put the Special Conference proposal to the vote, resulting in twenty-one votes for and three against, the latter being Ken Toon, Jack Jones and myself. Ray Chadburn immediately started to apply pressure to the three of us to get what he called unanimity in the Executive.

Ken Toon retaliated quite simply and directly: 'I do not agree that any decision here outweighs the decision at the Annual Conference which was to have a ballot vote.'

Ken, of course, was quite right.

Arthur then put to the meeting the amendment to change Rule 43 to a simple majority in a ballot vote, resulting again in twenty-one votes to three, the three against the amendment being, yet again, myself, Ken Toon and Jack Jones.

The meeting was closed, but not before Jack Jones had a parting shot: 'If my resolution is out of order here today, then the same resolution must be out of order at the Special Delegate Conference.'

That night Arthur was shown on the television screens, leaning out of a window of the NUM headquarters, speaking with a loud hailer to the cheering, chanting lobbyists below. The cheers grew louder as he announced: 'We intend to continue this fight until MacGregor and Thatcher withdraw their threats to our pits and our jobs.'

– 6 –

'Scargill's Army'

Britain was now seeing the flying picket as never seen before. Thousands of men, nicknamed 'Scargill's Army', were sent to various parts of the country to prevent other pitmen going to work. Sooner or later violence was bound to erupt. Violent picketing had, in my view, been spawned by the undemocratic decision taken by the NUM Executive. Arthur Scargill, of course, blamed the police for the violence. That wasn't surprising. He could do little else because the men leading the picketing represented the heart of his support.

Areas seemed powerless to prevent the 'troops' crossing their boundaries. Many of the pickets *were* peaceful ordinary miners, but there were some who were hell-bent on trouble, and many men were attacked simply because they dared to try and go to work.

Such scenes continued for some months and seemed only to subside when the union began to run short of cash for such operations. There was also another reason. The flying pickets had to deal with rebellions in their own areas. Men in Scotland, Yorkshire and South Wales were sick of being dictated to and decided to go back to work.

I was now receiving daily reports of growing rifts within the branches between members who were working, those who were refusing to cross picket lines, and those who fully supported strike action.

A wide spectrum of attitudes prevailed, ranging from those who would never take industrial action, via those who would not strike without a ballot, to the extreme militants who would walk out at the drop of a hat.

Many not working were quite adamant that they should not be referred to as strikers. They were not going through picket lines not because they were on strike but purely because of their trade union principles.

The Power Group Executive were astounded by the NUM Executive deciding not to hold a ballot vote but to leave the decision-making to a Special Delegate Conference instead. After I had presented them with a report of my speech and outlined the arguments put forward by other NUM Executive members, they instructed me to send a resolution to Peter Heathfield for inclusion on the agenda of the Conference urging that a ballot be taken in support of strike action.

Many NUM officials were imploring working miners to strike until the outcome of the Special Conference when, it was claimed, a ballot vote would be secured. But the vast majority ignored such advice and the NCB reported that more men were returning to the pits.

The Conference was held in the City Memorial Hall, Sheffield, on 19 April. I attended with our Power Group delegates, Bob MacSporran and Joe Sanderson.

We were not surprised to see thousands of lobbyists from the various areas outside the hall but, fortunately, the Executive had previously decided that only delegates and staff were to be allowed into the Conference.

We were to hear later that violence had erupted, and sixty-eight arrests made, several more being detained in hospital. Claims and counter-claims as to who was responsible were made by both miners and police. No one was shocked by the incident; such events had now become just another regular ugly scene in a violent strike.

The first item on the Conference agenda was the alteration to Rule 43 to provide a simple majority in a ballot vote for national strike action instead of 55 per cent. Only the Nottinghamshire area spoke against the proposal, and in a card vote there were 187 votes in favour with 59 against. Northumberland area abstained with 2 votes.

Peter Heathfield then eloquently addressed the Conference – his first since being elected General Secretary – on the current situation in the industry. He spoke so eloquently, in fact, that I am certain most of those present could not fail to be impressed.

For me, though, the right of the members to ballot was doomed when he said:

> . . . while I recognize and acknowledge the principle of ballots, I hope that we are sincere and honest enough to recognize that a ballot should not be used and exercised as a veto to prevent people in other areas defending their jobs, because there are people making the sort of noises and the bullish kind of statements that in many ways seem to me to be creating an anti-trade union attitude within groups of men. Now, that is the road to ruin. That is the road to disaster.

Jack Jones spoke briefly on the situation, and concluded by saying: 'The question, Mr Chairman, is this . . . does the rule book mean anything? If it means nothing then the organization cannot retain its credibility.'

He then moved the resolution that the Executive conduct a national ballot.

Bernard Donaghy, the Lancashire delegate, put forward his area's call for a ballot with a strong recommendation for strike action. He also talked of confrontation between miners, saying that his area was split down the middle. 'Our forefathers fought too long to have one union and one industry to throw it away by fighting ourselves. We see that a ballot vote is the only way to unite our members behind one battle.'

Next, Bob MacSporran moved the Power Group resolution, which was seconded, surprisingly, by the cokemen's leader, Idwal Morgan, whose area council had apparently met and mandated him to do so.

There were various other speakers but Yorkshire's Jack Taylor put the final nail in the coffin, as far as a ballot was concerned. He said: 'I will tell you what worries me about ballots, and I do not want to be offensive to anybody because we have got enough problems. I will tell you what is up. We don't really trust you; we don't really trust you,' he repeated.

He obviously meant he did not trust the members to vote for strike action and that was why he did not want them to have the opportunity to express their wishes in a democratic way.

Arthur Scargill wound up the debate, saying: 'There is only

Happier days. I welcome NUM President Arthur Scargill, guest speaker at the
Power Group's weekend school in Stoke-on-Trent in the autumn of 1983. Also in the
picture is Bob MacSporran, the Group's President. That weekend I was to tell
Arthur of my intention to retire the following year

Pit craftsmen from Stoke-on-Trent in March 1984 before travelling to NUM
headquarters in Sheffield to demand a national ballot over the strike. Jim Dowling,
the Power Group's Vice-President, stands in the foreground

High drama as miners are split on the issue of the strike. (Left) Early morning pickets at Florence Colliery, Stoke-on-Trent, are forced back by police. Pickets later complained that the police went too far. (Opposite) Coaches blaze in a bus depot in Stoke. They had been used to take miners to work in North Staffordshire

Left: I leave Silverdale Colliery, North Staffordshire, 29 March 1984, trying not to show the fear I feel inside. The face of the man behind me sums up the mood of the moment. I was taunted by jeering, spitting miners for organizing a meeting of some members of the NUM Executive to try to obtain a ballot over the strike

NCB Chairman, Ian MacGregor. I found him quite approachable, but it was always obvious his appointment would prove unpopular

Arthur addressing thousands of cheering strikers from the eighth floor of the NUM headquarters in Sheffield. This unforgettable scene followed the National Executive Committee meeting of 12 April when, for me, any hope of a ballot was destroyed. Also leaning out of the window is NUM Vice-President, Mick McGahey

Opposite: Arthur outside the Law Courts in the Aldwych, London, 23 May 1984, after three Nottinghamshire miners had taken High Court action over the legality of the strike call. 'No matter what the judges have said or will say, the decisions of this Conference are sacrosanct,' Arthur had said in his presidential address on 5 July 1982

All alone. Pondering on what is going to happen to the union, I look out of the
window of my office in the Power Group headquarters, Stoke-on-Trent, shortly after
resigning from the NUM Executive in October 1984

one rule, in my view, above all rules in that book, and that is when workers are involved in action, you do not cross picket lines under any circumstances.'

Not surprisingly, a resolution from the Kent area against a ballot carried the day. They got it by 69 votes to 51, at least the same 69 votes being cast against all resolutions calling for a ballot. It reaffirmed the decisions of the NUM Executive on 8 March and 12 April sanctioning strike action in areas under Rule 41.

It also called upon all areas to join the strike and, perhaps most important of all to the militants, stated that, in order to have as much unity as possible, future deployment of picketing and requests for solidarity action should be co-ordinated by the NUM head office.

The divisions within the Power Group became even greater when, due to the Kent area resolution becoming national policy, the Power Group Executive 'instructed' the members not to cross picket lines as opposed to previously 'advising' them not to do so.

Nevertheless, when the NUM's newspaper, the *Miner*, claimed in a front-page article on 30 April that 'the miners' strike is now a fully official national stoppage', my Executive strongly challenged the statement in a letter to Arthur Scargill, pointing out that a national strike could only be entered into as a result of a national ballot.

For me it was a time for reflection and analysis. I had told Arthur Scargill in October 1983 that I intended to retire soon.

Arthur had accepted an invitation to address Power Group delegates and the Executive at a weekend school in Hanley. It was lunchtime on Sunday, and we were having pre-lunch drinks at the bar of the hotel. I bought Arthur and the others a drink. I had a gin and tonic. Arthur had something less potent, as always – I've never known him drink to any degree. I remember him saying: 'Well, Roy,' in his usual friendly manner, 'how are things with you? I don't mean the job, but you yourself.'

'To tell you the truth, Arthur,' I replied, 'I've had enough, I'm ready to go. Obviously I would like to see the Power Group carry on, but I shall go when I reach sixty next November. Doris's illness [my wife had been seriously ill for some time] has made me even stronger in my resolve, and I shall need to talk to you in the future.'

'You must, Roy. Don't do anything until you have. July is an important date; we make calculations around then on inflation factors and so forth. I can understand your decision.'

Since then, in addition to the pressures of work, Doris's illness had caused me even more concern, convincing me that more of my time should be given to our lives together.

I informed Power Group President Bob MacSporran and Vice-President Jim Dowling of my decision on 30 April and on 8 May notified all branches by letter. I confirmed the decision with Arthur Scargill and Peter Heathfield, and the NUM Executive agreed to my retiring on 8 November 1984, my six-tieth birthday.

It was absolutely obvious now that there would be no ballot. At one point I began to wonder whether I was deluding myself and whether, after all, I should be whole-heartedly supporting the strike as a means to resolve the miners' and the industry's problems.

Of course I was concerned about pit closures; of course I was concerned about unemployment and job losses; and of course it was incumbent upon me to exercise what influence I had to resolve the problems. But, however one analysed the circumstances, I could not see that the course now confirmed by the Special Delegate Conference, with the inevitable internal factions embroiled in mutually destructive warfare, would bring about a better future for miners.

It was becoming increasingly clear that the strike might drag on for months. However, hopes were raised when a meeting was arranged for 23 May with NCB Chairman Ian Mac-Gregor and his team.

These first so-called 'peace talks' had been difficult to organize because of the perpetual presence of a picket line outside NCB headquarters in London. Finally the difficulty was resolved and Peter Heathfield confirmed that the NUM Executive would attend, but 'would reiterate at that meeting their demand for the pit closure programme to be withdrawn'. He emphasized that there could be no settlement of the dispute until this was done – a statement which did not bode well for the success of the talks.

The NUM Executive met for a short period before the NCB representatives joined us. Arthur Scargill had briefed us, reiterating that we would not be prepared to discuss the situation in the industry. We should listen, and then ask whether the NCB were prepared to withdraw the pit closures. We should consider what we would do if they refused.

'I am prepared to stay here for two days if the Board do that,' Arthur continued.

Mick McGahey said he was happy with the way the strike was growing and said that the NUM Executive should give consideration to a lobby of Parliament. There should be a demonstration, he said, about jobs, pit closures and the economy. Out of these words came the inspiration for the lobby of Parliament which was eventually held on 7 June, and was attended by thousands.

The NCB now joined the meeting, Ian MacGregor arriving last and taking the Chair. The mood of the meeting can best be judged by the fact that, just before his arrival, Mick McGahey made some taunting remark across the tables about the appointment of the septuagenarian MacGregor. Jim Cowan, Deputy Chairman of the NCB, had retorted: 'Imagine leaving the industry to you – an even worse disaster.'

The meeting started, Ian MacGregor saying that it would be useful to start with the industry's plans for the future and to review the 'Plan for Coal' document.

'Plan for Coal' is the name given to the Coal Industry Examination, which was set up by the Labour Government and introduced by Eric Varley in 1974 when he was Secretary of State for Energy. The plan had been widely welcomed and agreed by the tripartite body of the Government, the NCB and all unions involved in the industry.

Wishing to be as well-prepared as possible, I had brought a copy of 'Plan for Coal' with me, and had spent some time studying paragraph 27 about the mobility of labour.

It is worth citing some of it here:

> With the transformed outlook for coal ... the need to close pits on economic grounds should be much reduced. But inevitably some pits will have to close as their useful economic reserves of coal are depleted. The Board will make every effort to make local use of the valuable pool of trained and experienced manpower which will result from such closures. But where this is not possible the Board will take all reasonable steps to facilitate and assist the transfer of men who can move to other areas. We are glad to note that it has recently been agreed to improve the arrangements designed to safeguard the pay levels of men on transfer.

In short, it conflicted directly with the NUM's stance of opposing all economic closures.

The NCB reviewed 'Plan for Coal' and the current situation, ending with the statement that 'the plan remains to build a new industry from the old'.

Asked by Ian MacGregor if the NUM had any questions, the reply was 'no'.

The NCB then similarly dealt with the marketing aspects and problems.

Again no questions.

The NCB then presented the financial details, a loss of £875 million being projected for 1984–5.

'No questions,' replied the NUM.

The NCB next turned to the current state of the industry, in particular the effects that the NUM's action was having on the pits, the state of coalfaces and roadways and the risk of fires due to spontaneous combustion. Jim Cowan finally said: 'There is a need to talk to our colleagues opposite as to how we protect our assets. We on the Board remain ready to talk, but we need to make some decisions.'

Arthur Scargill said it was commonly agreed that the industry was in crisis, but that 'Mr MacGregor's statement to close 20 pits and lose 20,000 jobs created the crisis.' He went on to say that the further statement to remove more capacity had made it worse and that neither was in the 'Plan for Coal'. The only way to resolve the problems was for the NCB to withdraw their unilateral decision and then we could talk about the future of the industry. 'Are you prepared, Chairman, to withdraw?' he asked directly.

Ian MacGregor replied: 'I have no comment.'

Jim Cowan asked: 'Did I understand you were prepared to discuss proposals?'

Arthur Scargill reiterated that the only way to resolve the issues was to withdraw the 6 March statement to close 20 pits with 20,000 jobs this year: 'We can then talk about expansion.'

Jim Cowan then said: 'If there is any chance that Mr Scargill, Mr McGahey and Mr Heathfield are prepared to sit down and discuss the future within the "Plan for Coal", then we will do it.'

Mick McGahey said something, inaudible to me, but, Ian MacGregor replied, 'I retain my options like you retain yours.'

Jim Cowan spoke again: 'I said I am prepared to have discussions on the realities of the situation, producing 100 million tonnes, not at £70 per tonne against £35.'

Arthur Scargill said his suggestion had one flaw: the NCB's announcement.

Ian MacGregor said he would be happy to state where it was in 'Plan for Coal' and that he would meet Arthur personally.

Ned Smith, the Board's Industrial Relations Director General, then entered the discussion, saying that the 'Plan for Coal' did refer to closures on economic grounds: 'The proposals on 6 March', he said, 'were put by the Board after we had been asked to make the proposals.'

Arthur again said the NCB had made the announcement and the section of 'Plan for Coal' did not talk about closures on economic grounds, only exhaustion.

'These points don't advance us in reality,' said Ned Smith, 'and it seems to me if you are not prepared to move from that it is not very helpful.'

Jim Cowan then said, 'My offer remains on the table, to meet the national officials to discuss the future on the "Plan for Coal".'

But Arthur repeated his demand for the withdrawal of closures and loss of jobs.

The meeting ended when Mr MacGregor said: 'Thank you for coming. You have had the offer.'

There followed a meeting of the NUM Executive during which there were accusations and counter-accusations about working miners in Nottinghamshire. Coal was being transported by rail and organized by some officials, and officials were also in some cases encouraging men to work. One official said that 'People are saying they don't want to belong to the union, they want one of their own. What are we going to do?'

The NCB's attitude was deplored and reference made to action in the courts by working Nottinghamshire miners that day, Arthur Scargill saying that all we wanted was a degree of unanimity.

I immediately said that one thing I felt the members were unanimous upon was the need for the union to be talking to the NCB. I didn't care if it was just the three NUM officials, but I was concerned about the reaction of the members. Mick MacGahey simply said, 'You can't ask us to do that,' and the same was said by Peter Heathfield who said, 'It would be headlines tomorrow – "Scargill agrees to talk about pit closures – MacGregor stands firm". We can't talk about anything.'

The two sides, however, did finally meet but, despite hours and hours of discussion between the NCB and the three NUM officials, there was no agreement. The NUM remained adamant on no closures on economic grounds while the NCB stood firm and equally determined to retain their managerial responsibilities.

By now 75 per cent of the Power Group's 6,000 members were back at work. Many of them had not come out on strike at all, and many were returning who had previously not been prepared to cross picket lines, or had been too afraid to do so because of the ferocity of picketing.

Information was arriving at the office almost daily about incidents in which members had been arrested for various offences. One branch secretary, even though he was not working, kept on finding a waste skip dumped in his driveway – a present from 'friends'.

Families were rent by the effects of the method of action determined on that fateful 8 March. I was distressed to meet a striker one day in the office and the next day his working brother, both vowing never to speak to each other again.

Venomous hatred developed out of this civil war, not least because the strikers could see that whilst they and their families were suffering all the deprivations which came from no wages, working miners were able to continue the lives they had previously enjoyed.

It was even apparent on my own Executive, with four on strike and three working. I certainly knew how the strikers felt because NUM officials were not receiving wages – the NUM Executive had decided that soon after the strike started.

How different it all could have been if the rules of the union had been applied, a ballot vote held, and all members, as on previous occasions, abided by the result. How can a man, exercising the right given to him in a ballot in his own area, be called a 'scab' if he abides by the result and goes to work? After all, the members are the union, not the officials and leaders.

If the result of a ballot had been to strike, even with the simple majority required by the now changed rule, there would have been few, if any, so-called 'scabs', and greater support from the trade union movement, who had long held the NUM system of balloting in esteem.

In terms of supporting strike action there had been little prolonged support from the rank-and-file members of the other unions. This was made quite clear when the NUM Executive met the Executive of the Iron and Steel Trades Confederation. Bill Sirs, the General Secretary, remained firm in the belief that it was his Executive's responsibility to protect the jobs of their members despite all the picketing of steel plants throughout the country.

Such picketing was now organized from the NUM head office and, in any case, was really the responsibility of those areas where strikes had been sanctioned. My own area had not officially organized picketing in any way.

As the weeks went by, attitudes hardened considerably. It was no surprise when lobbyists gathered again outside the Power Group office on the morning of 19 June, waiting for Executive members to arrive for their meeting at 9.30 am. When the meeting opened, Bob MacSporran indicated to the

Executive that a request had been made by the lobbyists to meet them in order to express their views before the meeting.

It was thus agreed that four lobbyists be allowed to do so. Joining the meeting, each of the four accused the Executive councillors of sitting on the fence and told them it was time to support those members who were on strike. The Power Group area should be officially on strike, they said, and sanction sought from the NUM Executive.

After they had left, and the requests discussed, the Executive agreed by four votes to two that we would apply under Rule 41 to make the Power Group area officially on strike.

I was the one who had to go and read the decision to the chanting crowd and I have to say it was the most humiliating experience in my whole union career. The lobbyists' chants changed to cheers as they listened.

I was astounded that such a decision could have been made, particularly when one of the four voting in favour was due to pick up his redundancy pay within three or four weeks on leaving the industry, and another was employed in ancillary work in the industry and had worked continuously throughout the strike. Even worse was the fact that 75 per cent of Power Group members were at work, we had not had a ballot and, if we did, it would be against strike action.

I wrote to Peter Heathfield with the request and, by 6 July, it was confirmed that in accordance with the NUM Executive decision of 8 March and the special conference of 19 April 1984, the industrial action within the Power Group area was endorsed as official.

Jim Dowling had spoken out in the Press immediately after the decision, expressing his opposition to it, despite the fact that he had not crossed a picket line and gone to work since 8 March. That was at least some consolation, but the reaction from working Power Group members became even more marked, with dozens of forms being received, contracting out of the political fund levy to the Labour Party. Many were still arriving on my retirement day. Some branches in South Derbyshire obtained legal opinion on the issue, but did not pursue it through the courts.

The next Conference of the NUM was held in Firth Hall, Sheffield University, on 11 and 12 July 1984. It called itself an Extraordinary Annual Conference, the normal one having been cancelled because of the strike.

The NUM Executive tried to introduce at this Conference new disciplinary rules on disqualification of members, branches, areas and removal of officers. Putting the proposal, Arthur quite correctly pointed out that this was not designed 'at the time of or during the course of the dispute', despite some members, in Nottinghamshire and the Power Group, feeling it was a way of dealing with 'scabs' and others not supporting strike action. The media had already dubbed the proposal the 'Star Chamber'.

Nottinghamshire working miners had gone so far as to institute legal action and an order was made in the High Court to declare null and void the changes in the disciplinary rules.

The Conference became the target of mass-lobbying and, as one who had been subjected to verbal abuse and worse, my heart was in my boots as I walked towards the entrance, expecting at any moment to be recognized. Perhaps I should consider myself lucky. Although being personally opposed to my Executive Council decision to make the Power Group area strike an official one, it apparently gave me immunity from the lobbyists.

Less fortunate, as I shall explain later, were my two colleagues, Jack Jones and Ken Toon. They are both big and burly, but still older than me, Ken being the longest-serving NUM Executive member, twelve months longer than myself. Both were representing the views of their members, expressed in a ballot vote in Leicestershire and South Derbyshire, and their members were continuing to work.

After the presidential address, George Rees addressed conference as Chairman of the Business Arrangements Committee. He said that he did not wish to take advantage of the Chair, but he wanted to make it clear that South Wales would stick by its principle that they would not sit in the same room as scabs. He was speaking here to the people of South Derbyshire and Leicestershire. He would be staying in the Conference to cast the South Wales vote but he considered that people who said they were justified in sitting there when they had crossed picket lines, and witnessed the brutality of the police to the members, must have skins thicker than a rhinoceros.

The South Wales delegation consisted of ten people plus Emlyn Williams, General Secretary. They sat in the corridors outside the conference hall for the whole of the first day as well as the following morning.

When Ken Toon courageously went to the rostrum during the debate on the situation in the industry, he told delegates they would be entitled to call him a mouse if he didn't speak out in support of his area.

Most of the other delegates left the room including myself, accompanying my own delegates, and Ken ended up saying his piece to an almost empty room. It was later reported that he concluded by saying that it concerned him that the delegates had left the room and it was damaging the union. 'So where people have gone out of the room because of my area,' he said, 'I now invite them to come in because my delegation is going out and allowing the Conference to function as it should do.'

Ken bore me no malice and understood I went out in an act of unity with my own delegates. But I was not proud of my action and, on reflection, I should have stayed and given him moral support. Ken showed great tolerance but little was shown to him.

Later, when sitting having refreshments with Bob MacSporran at lunchtime, we heard that some young lobbyists had been asking for a description of Ken. We immediately realized the danger he was in and Bob shot off to warn him. I later saw the car in which Ken and Jack Jones were travelling being kicked and punched by young ruffians as it left the car park. Once again I was cruelly reminded of how low some of the NUM followers were sinking.

Because of the High Court decision to declare null and void the change in the disciplinary rules, a further conference had to be held on 10 August, all areas by this time having consulted their members on the proposed change. Again Arthur Scargill said: 'I simply make the point that it is not the intention of the

National Executive to hold a witch hunt against any individual branch or area of this union.' The lobbyists were there again and I am sure they had different ideas.

Power Group branches had mandated our delegates to vote against the proposals, but they were carried overwhelmingly by 167 votes to 22.

Jack Jones was to be under fire again shortly afterwards when at the NUM Executive meeting on 30 August the South Wales area had submitted a letter calling for his dismissal and his resignation from the Executive.

Arthur Scargill ruled that the NUM Executive could not dismiss Jack, but it didn't stop the left wing carrying a resolution for Jack to resign. I had expressed my views and called for everybody to exercise tolerance, but there was little of that about.

Jack's offence was that he had been seen on television at the new Vale of Belvoir coalfield, which was to provide jobs in due course for the Leicestershire miners, helping Ian MacGregor to knock in the first stake where development would start. In fact they were even holding the same hammer. There had also been some remarks exchanged, doubtless critical, about the NUM President.

Jack didn't resign, just as at the meeting I said he would not. But I couldn't help wondering what they would have done to me if they had seen the photograph of me taken with Ian Mac-Gregor at a meeting at my old pit, Bagworth, which he had visited on 21 November 1983.

By now it was 3 September, Trade Union Congress week.

The NUM Executive met and received information on the state of play with the TUC General Council. Looking back, it was all rather meaningless. True, there had been some excitement when, passing through the hordes of pressmen and television camera crews, we had sat down to debate the message proposing talks received from the NCB. But despite talks being developed with the NUM and the NCB, in the end they came to nought. NACODS were in the throes of argument with the NCB, which led to a ballot vote by their members in favour of striking. Action, however, was prevented by a negotiated settlement with the NCB. Arthur made an emotive address to delegates, received with rapturous applause, but the outcome was certainly not effective action in support of the strike by rank-and-file trade unionists in other industries. And the statement of the TUC General Council became more a basis for continuous talking. However, as stated before, the talks came to nought.

But for me, the most significant meeting of the week was a chance encounter on the first floor of the staircase leading to the Hotel Curzon bedrooms, where I was staying, along with Arthur and the head office entourage.

I walked up the staircase, and came to the entrance to the room which had been reserved as an office for the NUM. Outside the door stood Nell Myers. Nell is the NUM Press Officer and a most pleasant girl – always courteous, respectful and ready to assist in any problems that one might have. No one would doubt her commitment to the cause as pursued by the NUM leadership.

'Hello Mr Ottey, how are you?' she cried out, as friendly as ever.

'I don't know, Nell,' I said, 'I am concerned as to where we are going.'

I told her how I had suffered in my young days from the consequences of the 1926 strike, and, more particularly, the aftermath. 'We were paupers, bloody poor, and it hurts me to think of the miners and their families who are now suffering in the same way,' I said.

I ranted on, saying we were here in a fine hotel, sitting down to excellent meals, having bottles of the best wines while the lads in the field enjoyed none of these pleasures.

'I know,' she said, 'but. . .'

Somewhat discourteously, I interrupted, quoting the story of one of our lads who the week before had taken his shoes off to give to one of his mates who hadn't got any.

'Do you wonder, Nell, if I ask myself now what the hell I've achieved?'

I stopped to let her speak. She asked me to think of the minds that had awakened to the political reality and how many now understood the battle which had to be fought and won.

I was not surprised by her words but they didn't exactly help to cheer me up. There was little point in pursuing the discussion. 'Nell, that's not the way I ended up thinking. It made me go the other way,' I said, and went off up the stairs to bed.

There were to be three NUM Executive meetings in September, one even on a Sunday, all largely dealing with the talks which were proceeding with the NCB and TUC, and keeping abreast of the NACODS dispute. Throughout these I felt there was growing unease about what was being achieved. After all, the strike had now gone on longer than that in 1926. I remember on one occasion hearing Arthur, before opening the meeting at the other end of the room, using his favourite word 'devastating' about some happening or document. Someone at the opposite end had riposted: 'Everything's "devastating", to hear him talk, but there's no settlement.' Then Jack Taylor, characteristically straightforward in a typical Yorkshire manner, said: 'We've won nowt yet,' and, in one of his speeches, had made reference to the possibility of a pending court action by some of his members. 'If the strike is declared unofficial, it will cause a break in the lines,' he warned.

Even Peter Heathfield agreed, saying that holding the line would be difficult. There had been no impact from the strike; the lights hadn't gone out and primarily this was due to miners working in Leicester, South Derbyshire and Nottinghamshire.

Of course, in his usual, irrepressible fashion, Arthur disagreed with Peter. There had been an impact, he argued, and he was 'optimistic of winning'.

In line with my own thinking was the whispered observation from a colleague as he passed behind me at the end of the meeting, 'We're up a cul-de-sac, Roy.'

It had also been worrying to hear Ray Chadburn saying we were in a mess. He was referring specifically to the legal steps being taken by working miners in Nottinghamshire to disentangle the area rules from national rules, with the intention, it was thought, of removing two of the officials. Five thousand had also withdrawn from the political levy. No doubt the 'mess' was not helped by the new disciplinary rules.

I drove to the Winter Gardens in Blackpool for the Labour Party Conference on Sunday, 30 September 1984 with my colleague Joe Sanderson, who was the Power Group delegate to Conference. Of course, the conversation revolved about the strike, the delegation meeting and what the week might hold for us.

The meeting passed, like others before, with attitudes to resolutions being decided, as well as who should speak for the various resolutions, before conference. There was little here of consequence or significance, when set beside the burden we carried of the miners' strike. Arthur made another rapturous speech, and the same rapturous support was given.

During the Monday afternoon session, Eric Heffer, Chairman of Conference, made the announcement, with critical contempt, that some person had served a writ during the Conference proceedings on Arthur Scargill, 'he to be subject to execution', a play upon the content of the actual writ.

For various reasons, Conference continued well past the stipulated time for closure of 5 pm.

By the time the delegation had dealt with what is known as the composite resolutions – resolutions which overlap but which come from different sources – it must have been about 6.45 pm. The NUM Executive members were requested to stay behind.

Arthur then informed us that a writ had been served on him, Peter Heathfield and Mick McGahey. There had also been writs, although of a different kind, served on the Yorkshire and North Derbyshire areas.

Arthur explained that the writ related to a statement he had made on Channel 4 television news. This statement was alleged to be a contempt of the judge's ruling in the case taken by Robert Taylor and Kenneth Foulstone, members of the Yorkshire area. They were two miners who believed that the strike in Yorkshire was unofficial.

Arthur went on to propose a statement which, in effect, committed the Executive to support the statement he had made on Channel 4.

I interrupted and said as far as I was concerned, my area, the

Power Group, just like Taylor and Foulstone, had contested the claim that the strike was an official strike. I explained that when this was stated in an issue of the *Miner* we wrote to Peter Heathfield and challenged it. Furthermore, the Power Group, albeit by Executive decision, had asked that the area be on official strike. This had been endorsed by the NUM Executive, but the fact remained that the area, and any other area, was only on strike under Rule 41.

'Yes, Roy,' said Arthur, 'we will write that into the statement, "The strike is under Rule 41."'

The meeting closed, all present wanting to get away to their respective hotels for dinner.

I returned to conference next morning, showing my delegation card at the stewards' barrier. Through the barrier, I suddenly saw Arthur, standing before the television cameras, explaining something. I passed by, and as I walked towards the conference hall, I was joined by Nell Myers who had apparently broken away from the television crew as I had walked by.

'Good morning, Mr Ottey,' she said, 'How are you today?'

'Well, Nell,' said I, 'I am not at all happy, I haven't seen the writ, I didn't see the judgement and I didn't hear Arthur's statement on Channel 4. And yet, we are asked to make a decision. I am not happy at all.'

'I know,' said Nell, 'I am just going off to knock out a statement which will be handed out to the NEC this morning.'

'Oh, good,' said I. She left and walked on into Conference.

Suddenly Arthur came up beside me, having obviously finished the interview. He was his usual friendly, animated self.

'I can't understand it, Roy! You know I don't want to operate Rule 51 [the disciplinary rule which was introduced in August], that's not my intention, I don't want to take anybody under it.'

'That's not the point,' I replied. 'Whether you want to or not, there are many who do now that it is in the rule book. We have applications from many already in our area.

'But that is not the issue at the moment. Nell tells me she is knocking out a statement this morning for the NEC, but I haven't seen the writ, the judgement, nor the statement you made on Channel 4. How can I make a decision on that basis?'

'I'll show you the writ,' said Arthur, motioning me towards a radiator. He placed his red briefcase on it, clicking open the catches and opening the lid.

'Well, well,' he said as it opened. 'Nell's got it.'

There was only an empty brown envelope inside.

'Never mind, Arthur,' I said, 'I will see the statement when it's ready.'

I took my seat amongst the delegates and listened to the Conference debates. There were three or four seats empty in the row in front of the one in which I was sitting, and Trevor Bell was sitting in the one in front of that. Suddenly Arthur appeared and sat down in one of the empty seats, a sheaf of papers in his hands. Turning round, he handed one paper to me, one to Trevor Bell and then one to Ted McKay.

I read it. It said:

> Following discussion, the NEC unanimously agreed to: fully endorse and support the view expressed by the National President during an interview on Channel 4 television news last Friday September 28, 1984: that no High Court Judge will take away the democratic right of our union to deal with internal affairs, such as crossing a picket line or urging others to cross a picket line in defiance of our union's instructions, and to reaffirm as official strike action in the coalfields sanctioned in accordance with National Rule 41 as determined by the Special National Delegate Conference on April 19, 1984, the Extraordinary Annual Conference and the National Executive Committee.

'I can't accept this Arthur, no way,' I said, 'If the statement read "should take away" instead of "will take away" it might be different, but I can't accept it like that.'

He waffled on and, while he did, Trevor Bell and I emphasized again that the statement was not acceptable.

Arthur went back to his seat at the end of the row. Trevor and I left and went to the Planet Room, a large room in the basement of the building, for coffee and a talk. Bob MacSporran, Jim Dowling and Joe Sanderson were there, watching the proceedings on closed circuit television. I showed them the document, pointing out the offending words, and said that I couldn't accept it.

'Surely,' said Bob, 'you don't think that Arthur should go to gaol, do you, Roy?'

Of course I didn't think Arthur should go to gaol, but that was not the point. He didn't need to. I told Bob: 'He didn't come to us, the NEC, and ask our opinion on the judgement. He simply goes straight on to television and commits the contempt. All he has to do is purge his contempt between now and next Wednesday and gaol doesn't enter into it. I haven't seen the writ, the judgement or the television statement and I am not going along with it.'

Bob was not at all happy with my attitude, of that I am sure.

I went back into Conference, Trevor Bell was back in his seat. We agreed there ought to be a meeting of the full NUM Executive. 'I'm going to have a word with him and tell him so,' said Trevor. He went down the row in front of the delegates. Then I saw him squatting in the aisle talking to Arthur.

He came back, and sat down in front of me. 'I've told him we ought to have a meeting, Roy, and that a lot of us are not happy with the situation, but he says leave it for the moment, the TGWU are going to develop a resolution to place before Conference, calling for total support for the NUM against the writs.'

I couldn't believe it. Conference would never do it. The whole Labour movement would be pledged to committing contempt of the law. Well, whatever happened, I would not!

Delegates were all back in their seats early after lunch, the visitors' gallery full, anticipating the speech to be made by Neil Kinnock, Leader of the Labour Party.

Word buzzed around that the TGWU were not now to move the suggested resolution but would be making a statement of their own position which it was hoped could gain support.

I had to return home that day, and during the speech in which Neil Kinnock condemned violence – a good speech, I thought – I was on edge because my time would be up on the car park ticket I had bought.

Immediately the speech and standing ovation ended, I passed down the row of delegates to leave. I went to Arthur, sitting

TS - 6

at the end of the row in front, and placed my hand on his arm. 'Arthur, I have to go home because Doris has to go into hospital in the morning. Are we going to have any meetings of the NEC?'

'No,' he said abruptly, shaking his head.

I drove home, preoccupied with thoughts of the hospital.

Doris was to report for treatment by a neurologist to remove, or at least minimize, the considerable pain she was suffering from scarred tissue and nerves, the result of a previous course of radio-therapy. In the event, her stay had to be overnight. This prevented my return to Conference on the Thursday morning. Back home that night, we briefly talked of the contempt of the law.

'I think I'll ring Trevor. I know he was going home from Conference tonight.'

'I should,' she said.

Trevor was home, and together we relived the events of Conference. He confirmed that the TGWU statement had been made but fell far short of Conference supporting contempt of the law.

I conveyed my view that something positive needed to be done, and Trevor was of the opinion that at the NUM Executive meeting to be held the following Thursday we could challenge the minutes of the meeting which had been held on the Monday night of conference week.

'But that's too late,' I said, 'Justice Nicholls will be making his decision on Wednesday, the day before, and we shall all have broken the law or have been in contempt of it by then.'

We ended our conversation.

The following days brought much turmoil of the mind, culminating in my reaching a crucial decision. I outlined it to Doris. There was nothing for it: I would resign from the NUM Executive. I had never knowingly broken the law and I wasn't going to start at this stage of my life, certainly not to please or support Arthur Scargill who hadn't had the courtesy, even less the humility, to ask us lesser Executive mortals for our opinion.

I went to the office to confirm details, and wrote my letter of resignation.

Bob MacSporran rang during the afternoon to let me know that, running contrary to all his previous decisions, for he had been on the point of taking redundancy and going back to Scotland, he had accepted nomination by his branch for the vacancy on the NUM Executive which would occur on my retirement.

'I am resigning tomorrow from the NEC. I'll be sending a copy of my letter to all our branch and unit secretaries and reporting to our Executive Council at their meeting on Tuesday morning,' I told him.

'I can't say I blame you,' he replied.

– 7 –
I Resign

Once again I found myself at the centre of controversy. The local evening paper told their readers: PIT CHIEF IN I QUIT NEC SHOCK. That night I was featured on television, and the following morning the national Press analysed what effect my decision would have on the left- and right-wing tussle on the NUM Executive.

Of course, much was made of the fact that I was a magistrate and was therefore not prepared to break the law, and the Press pointed out that my action followed the controversial NUM Executive contempt of court ruling at Blackpool. 'I have been unhappy for some time, and this was the last straw,' I was quoted as saying. 'I am not prepared to back Arthur Scargill's defiance of the High Court.'

And so on 8 October 1984 I resigned from the NUM Executive. The following month it would have been eighteen years that I had served on the NUM's ruling body. But in my mind I had no alternative: I had to resign.

I felt, though, as if I was departing the family I had helped to create. I had spent forty-four years in the union; my two grandfathers, my father, my father-in-law, three brothers-in-law, eight uncles and at least four cousins had all been union men – some of them had fifty-two years in service, many of them working underground.

I was certain that my action reflected the majority view of Power Group members – the bulk of whom were going to work – and in my letter of resignation to Arthur Scargill I reminded him of my constant opposition to the sanction of the area strikes, my support for a ballot and my forecast of civil war throughout the coalfields.

When I wrote to Arthur I attached a copy of the original letter in which the Power Group challenged the statement that the miners' strike was a national official stoppage. I told him that 80 per cent of the Group's members were working and, finally, that my decision to resign was to disassociate myself from defying the judicial procedures, implemented by members who only really wanted a democratic ballot vote.

Arthur's reply, setting out in detail the offending statement and procedures leading to it, ended by telling me that I had had 'a change of heart' and had decided 'inexplicably to take a different view to the one which was supported unanimously by the NEC on 1 October'.

He knew that it was not a unanimous decision and I had told him quite plainly at Blackpool that I could not back such a decision. But what can one say to the man? I simply acknowledged the letter, reminded him of what actually happened, and set out the resolution by the Power Group Executive supporting my stand. I asked him to convey my appreciation to my colleagues on the Executive for their friendship, help and experience over the years.

Some members of the NUM Executive did telephone and congratulate me on my decision, in particular that tough character from my home town, Jack Jones, who simply said 'Good lad' before I set off again to argue my case on BBC's programme, 'Newsnight' and the following day on TV-am.

One of my colleagues on the Executive wrote much later, in answer to a letter I had sent him wishing all the best for his future. He said he had no grudge against me whatsoever, his only misgiving being that I had publicized the event in the Press and on television.

How naive he was. He should have realized I had no alternative, for there were members on the Executive who hated my guts, and if they had been left to make the announcement they would have put their own slant on my resignation. It was important I got in first.

It was easy enough for the situation to be twisted. Arthur Scargill was reported in the *Daily Mail* as saying:

Mr Ottey's statement about his resignation is actually astonishing given the fact that his own area [the Power Group] is on official strike and that since April 19 he has consistently supported this official strike action.

It was obvious that I would be shunned by some who considered I had turned my back on the union which was fighting to preserve pits and jobs. But I am convinced I made the right decision. The union was in a sorry state. The fact that members were going to law for basic democracy demonstrated the failure of the NUM to provide proper leadership.

The Power Group Executive at their next meeting said that they fully supported 'the personal principled stand' I had taken, and unanimously endorsed my decision to resign.

I was grateful and touched, but sad that I had had to resign with only four weeks to go to retirement. I was equally grateful and touched by the generous gesture they made, giving me an ex-gratia payment in recognition of my twenty-five years' service as an official of the union.

Somehow, though, I still felt lonely, as though the decision I had made had chopped off a great part of my life. I missed all those members of the NUM Executive, whatever their political ideology, who had been friends and colleagues. Had I retired in the normal way, then at my final meeting, scheduled for my birthday on 8 November, the parting would have been entirely different.

My sadness was relieved a little some days later when two young strikers in Kent rang me at home at midnight to find out why I had resigned. They were courteous and friendly but they wanted to know, directly from me, exactly what I thought. We had a long discussion on the implications of the strike – they were ardent supporters and would remain so. But they fully understood my decision and my sadness at having to make it. I wrote to Jack Collins, with whom I had done battle about a ballot on BBC's 'Newsnight', asking him to thank the two young men on my behalf and wishing Jack and his family a good future. It hurt when I got no reply.

It also hurt, and I thought it out of character, when Arthur Scargill, as President of the union, did not express any sentiments whatsoever upon my retirement. Peter Heathfield did at least send me his best wishes when replying to another business letter.

Perhaps these actions played a part in motivating me to write this book. Many things did, not least the memory of Arthur Scargill's first presidential address. 'I would not compromise my policies,' he had said, 'nor prostitute my principles.'

Well, neither would I, and if Arthur believes in democracy, then he should accept that. Many working miners are standing by their principles too, as are the strikers. This division is an unnecessary blow to the union; democracy has not prevailed and Arthur Scargill could so easily have ruled for a ballot.

'I intend to work according to the rules in an open democratic way and will engage in no secret dealings,' said Arthur in the same address. 'I do not believe the membership can achieve any material gain from so-called secret diplomacy, but can in fact lose by being excluded from discussions.'

I totally agree with him, and by my writing this book, the members will certainly not be excluded from the Executive discussions which took place on that fateful day of 8 March. My Power Group Executive and the Group's members had the details anyway. Perhaps that is why 82 per cent of them are now at work?

Talking is better than fighting, and the 'new realism', which some apparently believe has now arrived, must be fostered if we are to avoid the damaging consequences which we have all suffered through the strike.

That, I am sure, was the approach adopted by Ned Smith, the NCB's Industrial Relations Director General, at the meeting on 23 May 1984 when rightly he had said, 'It is alright everybody scoring points but it doesn't help any of us. These points don't help us in reality. . . .'

The observation applied to all sides in the debate, for Ned was fully aware that at some stage the industry would be required to produce the coal the nation needed. To do this, there must be, in an industry like mining, total co-operation if the future is to be successful for all.

I have long felt that many changes had to be accepted if the industry is to move efficiently into the twenty-first century. It has become increasingly obvious over the years that new technology would bring down the numbers employed. One could, in fact, take the view that machinery *should* replace the arduous and hazardous jobs that had to be done. Once the machinery was installed, common interest demanded that there would be exploitation of the investment to achieve the maximum competitive output.

A Government minister some years ago impressed me with a speech which I shall never forget. He said that those who resist the application of new technology, whether they be old-fashioned management or short-sighted workers, were destroying the long-term future of this country. He also spoke about raising the level of efficiency 'so that we can increase the total sum of national wealth, so that we can provide the resources we need in order to ameliorate the consequences of these changes, and also provide new employment for those who have been displaced'.

The speaker was not an ex-NCB official or an industrialist, but Anthony Wedgwood Benn when he was Minister of Technology in 1967.

Addressing a TUC Conference, Tony Benn accepted that new technology resulted in serious human problems which would affect a large number of people but, quite rightly in my opinion, he added: 'There is in fact no choice for us. We have to press ahead and earn our living by our skill and our readiness to innovate.'

He went on about awakening the trade union leaders at every level, together with the rank and file, to the terrible waste of effort and ability without it.

He predicted attitudes adopted during the 1984 miners' strike, when he said: 'In short, the technological revolution is turning out to be a real revolution. Sometimes I have heard the word revolution used in the past in such an easy way that it suggested that we were going to be able to reorganize our society without any pain or misery attached to it.

'There are those who seem to think that we are destined to be sheltered from the harsh and unsettling disturbance that we have seen in other nations when they faced similar problems.'

It was as if he was looking into a crystal ball when he continued: 'The truth, I am afraid, is very different. Our technological revolution is a real revolution. The man who is thrown out of work by the new machine feels bitter and angry about it. The man who has been redeployed and retrained and is denied employment in his new skill is also bitter and angry.'

Extending what seems to be now a word of advice to the NCB as to what they should do about the industry, Tony Benn said: 'Productivity is not perhaps a very good word for us to use. What it means is getting more out of less – producing more goods with less human effort.'

He went on: 'The plain fact is that technology represents the one chance we have of lifting ourselves – all of us – to a higher living standard.'

I do, of course, appreciate that there are some significant differences in the current dispute, but it is certain that Tony Benn was, and still is, basically correct.

Correct too is the fact that the impact of harsh and unsettling disturbances likely to arise in the mining industry was cushioned by the guarantee that each miner was to have a job if he did not want to leave. If he decided to leave the industry because of the changes taking place, the redundancy payments would be the best in British industry.

How can I help but contrast this with the situation faced by many thousands throughout Britain who were forced to leave their jobs in the recession of the early 1980s with the minimum redundancy payment?

For its part, the NCB publicly announced the guarantees, together with a backdated 5.2 per cent pay offer and, in the full-page advertisements in national newspapers, highlighted the thousands of pounds lost by each striker in the dispute.

My last few weeks in office were not to be happy ones, especially when I surveyed the enormity of the divisions within the membership.

Over the years, although there were – and always would be – disagreements, I was sure I had created a small union totally committed to serving the members in the most democratic manner, providing them with maximum information through their branches, and primarily recognizing that each and every one of them was intelligent enough to have an opinion and be entitled to express it.

And, indeed, the Power Group had been a largely united family. But it was not so during my last few weeks in office; legal actions were being pursued by working members; branches were split asunder; there were allegations of unfair dealing in a ballot taking place to deal with the NUM Executive position I had created through my resignation, and tense relationships and frictions within the Power Group Executive.

Even on my last day but one, with the ballot results to be dealt with, the atmosphere could only be described as electric. Sparks were flying in all directions as a result of legal action being taken to contest the outcome.

The general problems faced by the Power Group were being repeated in other areas. It was sad to see that once great union, the NUM, whose members are stalwart supporters and the very backbone of the Labour movement and Labour Party, being split through internal troubles, and miners and their families suffering distress and deprivation, beset with attitudes and problems from which they may take years to recover – if ever.

I was sick at heart, and at the same time angry with those who had over the years advocated the policies which had resulted in this crisis. Those on the left who had previously had power without responsibility and had told members: 'If you had listened to us, you would have had more', seemed powerless to suggest anything other than: 'Stick it out on strike lads, suffer and we shall win in the end'.

To add insult to injury Arthur Scargill telephoned me on 19 October 1984 and questioned me as to whether I had divulged union documents to a firm of solicitors. These were court orders relating to the actions taken by Robert Taylor and Kenneth Foulstone, the NUM members in Yorkshire.

The Power Group solicitor, Michael McKnight, was with me at the time in my office and heard the conversation. I told

Arthur that Michael would speak to him and confirm the position. No correspondence had gone to the solicitors who had served the court orders; Michael had simply sent a letter protecting my position. Arthur seemed to lose interest and rang off. I immediately sent a letter to him, relating the events and confirming that no correspondence of the union had been divulged.

I heard no more about it but I couldn't help thinking that, despite what he was saying in public and to me personally at the Labour Party Conference, he was hoping to take disciplinary action against me under the new rules for the offence of divulging union documents.

The union seemed to be beset by a variety of legal problems and I could well understand why four former colleagues on the NUM Executive had reportedly appointed their own legal advisers rather than relying on the NUM. Action was taken in court to make each member of the NUM Executive personally liable to pay a share of the £200,000 contempt of court fine against the NUM and the four executive members were only looking after their own interests.

'Salting away' the funds may have provided much work for the sequestrators appointed by the court to seize NUM funds, but this put the union in great difficulty because it was unable to use its own money to run the organization. And what a price there must be to pay in costs – all coming from members' contributions.

My Power Group Executive had been proved right in ignoring the advice given to 'hide' the funds. Even I as an Executive member of the NUM did not know where the national funds had gone.

The middle of January 1985 saw the NUM in another deep constitutional crisis. The Nottinghamshire miners decided they would not capitulate to the anti-democratic forces which removed their right to an individual ballot vote. They divorced themselves from national rules and suspended their General Secretary, Henry Richardson. And using Roy Lynk, the area Finance Officer, as a mouthpiece, they said they were not going to be led by Arthur Scargill, whom they considered to be a tyrant.

All this turmoil takes me back where it all started for me nearly sixty years ago. The actions of today are in many ways similar to the events of the 1926 strike. My father, grandfather and uncles were all affected by the misery and poverty of that strike. Warring with their spouses due to lack of money and suffering the ignominy of crawling back to work, they also endured the split that occurred within the coalfields, not least the formation of the Nottinghamshire Spencer union, that breakaway union led by George Spencer which ultimately failed in its aims.

As if all this were not enough, I am now probably witnessing the beginning of the end of my own Power Group. Under the guise of implementing a 1983 Annual Conference decision, proposed by the South Wales area, several areas face the threat of being amalgamated and thus losing their identity.

One is bound to ask the question 'why'? It cannot be due to the economic position, because each area of the union runs its own financial affairs, making the required contribution to national funds, but, at the same time, ensuring that they have reserves available to protect their own autonomy. It is a well-known fact that the areas of the union combined are far richer than the NUM. In any case, I am sure that Arthur Scargill would not want to use that economic argument because it would be too much like the NCB projections on pit closures.

It is also a fact that my own Power Group on a per capita basis was equal to the best in the NUM, its profitability being on a par with the large Yorkshire and Nottinghamshire areas. So what is the reason? It is fair to suggest that the revision of rules, if not opposed by those areas to be removed from the scene, and if implemented, will give even greater emphasis to left-wing superiority on the NUM Executive.

How else can one justify the left-wing Kent area, with only 2,300 members, still having a representative on the Executive, while they propose expelling the Power Group, Leicestershire and South Derbyshire areas?

Well, I suppose Kent did support the strike action from day

one, and it was their resolutions which were ultimately to form NUM policy at subsequent conferences.

I am still acutely aware of the provocative way in which Kent's Jack Collins, in that debate with me on television, attempted to ridicule the Power Group's standing by suggesting that we were simply 'a few drivers who are not miners'. The opposite is the case, there being well over twice as many members in the Power Group, all highly trained technicians, electricians and mechanics, working at all levels in the pits from coalface to surface, and at workshops and research establishments.

Though my attitudes and opinions may count for little now, surely there will be someone who will take up the cudgels for democracy, dispel the untruths and uncover the manipulative practices that seem to become ever more prevalent. How I wish I was thirty again.

The words of a quotation: 'Advice is seldom welcome; and those who want it the most always want it the least,' echo inside my head. I believe the leadership of the NUM and the NCB ought to give time towards some new thinking with fresh ideas to preserve the future well-being of the industry.

And how about the strike? It has gone on almost a year now, and will probably go on many months longer if the trickle back to work does not become a flood. That is no way of retaining the dignity that miners have justifiably earned over the years. The proposals being considered for NUM Conference – unless the leadership has some grandiose master plan which I do not know about – can only lead to greater unrest with other areas arriving at the same decision as Nottinghamshire, and breaking away from the NUM. But time will tell all.

I know too that divisions have appeared and will no doubt remain within the NCB hierarchy. I am not the only person to have resigned on an issue of principle. Others in the NCB, mindful of the relationships that had been developed in the industry, have also gone, some of them senior executives.

Resolving the strike is a joint responsibility that should be shouldered and carried, and I can see no other means of achieving it than that leaders on all sides should be given new instructions to provide a new initiative.

I did propose an alternative to the appointment of Ian Mac-Gregor, who will, in any case, be unlikely to be reappointed when his present term of office expires in September 1986. I did propose an alternative to the election of Arthur Scargill by supporting Trevor Bell. It was to no avail, and Trevor will not be eligible again. But perhaps Arthur himself, who was elected for life and who made part of his election platform the re-election every five years of fulltime union officials, will also seek a new mandate by resigning and hoping for re-election.

Five years of presidency for him will cease in March 1987, very nearly coinciding with the end of Ian MacGregor's term of office. Perhaps they will go earlier, together? I meanwhile have already gone.

I retired from work on Thursday, 8 November. The weekend was bliss. Although my mind was still crammed full of problems – the strike, the NUM Executive position and the future of the Power Group – I was able to go into the greenhouse and the garden, and do all the little jobs in preparation for the retirement holiday in Tenerife – provided the neurologist at the hospital was prepared to let Doris go.

It was bliss: nobody telephoned except friends. There were none of the calls from pressmen, television or radio stations that had been an ever-present feature of weekends over the previous twelve months. I was not continuously being called in to the house, away from the relaxing jobs I so much like doing. On the other hand, though, I did resent it a bit: it was lonely; nobody wanted me now. Despite the many cards I had received on my retirement and birthday, and on my resignation from the Executive congratulating me on the stand I had taken, it was really a very lonely period.

Doris was permitted to take the holiday in Tenerife. There was beautiful sunshine when we arrived at the first port of call at lunchtime, the Frigate, the English pub in the Puerto de la Cruz's tiny harbour. I have to confess I do enjoy a pint of beer now and they sold John Smith's bitter.

A big man, smiling-faced, appeared at the next table. 'You know,' I said to him, 'you're the spitting image of Don Concannon, MP from Nottingham.'

Of course, it wasn't him but, within seconds, he had moved his belongings and drinks, and sat down with us at the table, and had recognized me. Des and his friend John, from Sheldon in Birmingham, had followed the events of the miners' strike on television and knew that I had resigned from the NUM Executive.

It turned out they were roof-tilers and builders, taking a well-earned relaxing two weeks' holiday. During our conversation on the strike they said they admired the principled stand I had taken in refusing to break the laws of Britain.

This chance meeting was to be the forerunner of many others, and walking slowly back to our hotel I did not feel lonely any more. Des and John were strangers, but to me they represented the salt of the earth like the miners I know.

The little girl I heard being interviewed on the radio was also a stranger. I had listened to her some three weeks before while driving in the car to the office. Her dad was on strike, like mine before him in 1926, and he had sold the video, the television and the car and was in arrears with the mortgage.

'There are a lot more rows in our house,' she said, 'always about money.'

The interviewer asked: 'Do you think strikes are good then?'

The little girl answered in a resoundingly loud voice, 'No.' Her words echoed my sentiments entirely as I watched my father play cards, staking bets with matches in the hot summer of 1926. . . .

Please God, make sure that at sixty she cannot tell a story about miners with an ending like mine.

Winding Up

Looking in from the outside, now just a member of the general public, I see the situation deteriorating for the union. Talks fail before they start; £5.4 million NUM assets have been seized by the sequestrators, and the £200,000 fine on the union for contempt of the law has now been paid as expected.

The talking has slowed the drift back to work, but if the peace talks fail, then the trickle could, once again, turn into a flood. We could soon reach the stage where over half the membership of the NUM is working, and the NCB declares the strike over.

There seem to be new developments every hour, with accusations flowing to and fro. The main sticking point, as always, is the closure of what the NCB term as 'grossly uneconomic' pits. The NCB want an assurance that the NUM will discuss loss-making collieries in the talks, otherwise they say the meetings will simply be a repeat performance of others, with the union not prepared to discuss what is, in fact, the heart of the dispute.

The union is insisting that everyone goes into the meeting without preconditions. The Prime Minister, Margaret Thatcher, is being accused of blocking peace talks and trying to destroy the NUM.

In fact, on this day, the union is no nearer a settlement than at the beginning of the strike, and the only hope for the NUM now appears to rest on possible support from other unions, and pressure being put on the Government by the TUC and Labour MPs.

It is noticeable that Ian MacGregor is adopting a low profile; he has delegated much to official spokesmen. Arthur Scargill is less buoyant and obviously less confident about the outcome. It seems a long time since he said coal stocks were low and the lights would start going out in the winter. But he is still fighting, and stresses: 'The NUM is not begging or crawling to the National Coal Board for a resumption of negotiations.' He does say, however, that he wants to see an end to the dispute in the interests of the miners and the country.

The past few days have been for me a period of reflection, my mind vividly recalling events over the last year or so, and the terrible burden that has been inflicted on both working and striking miners through no fault of their own. The blame must rest with the NUM Executive, and I share in that blame.

I hope that every mineworker will, in the future, take an active part in the union and insist that the rules are upheld. I also hope that everyone involved in the dispute today reminds themselves that the miners are the future of the industry, and their faith in it has got to be restored.

Recent statements by leaders of the union, the NCB and the Government, have been contrary to that concept, and they would do well to remember the words of George Bernard Shaw: 'It is easy – terribly easy – to shake a man's faith in himself. To take advantage of that to break a man's spirit is devil's work.'

Roy Ottey
4 February 1985

Index